This book reveals a miracle. The nation of Wales survives, strong and dynamic after centuries of oppression and neglect.

Most small nations have been swallowed up by their big neighbours. Not Wales. Against all odds Wales flourishes.

Here is an exciting romp through thousands of years of Welsh history. His-tory. Her-story. **Our**-story. This generation is fortunate to witness the fulfilment of the dreams and sacrifices of our forebears.

Without knowledge of the past, the present is meaningless. This book proves that vital knowledge is best conveyed with simplicity, lubricated with humour. With pride it lists the sacrifices, victories and failures of the nation's heroes.

This was not always the case. Generations of Welsh children were taught to ignore or despise their own history. Those educated in the last war were served a 'King and Empire First' distortion of British supremacy. Little or nothing was said of the brilliant leadership of Hywel Dda and Owain Glyndŵr. The martyrs Dic Penderyn and the Newport Chartists were dismissed as drunken troublemakers.

Now they have their honoured places as trailblazers. Many of our present prized values were pioneered in Wales. It was mediaeval Welsh Law that accorded women equal rights. The virtues of cooperation were proved by Robert Owen. The Chartists helped to shape our political ethics. Anuerin Bevan used the Tredegar experience as the model for the world's finest health service.

Not that it is possible to be certain on even recent history. Controversy still rages on the police charge on strikers in 1910. The Home Secretary responsible, Winston Churchill, claimed in 1951 that the miners were hit with 'rolled-up raincoats' not truncheons or firearms. The most wounding lesson in Welsh history is the treachery of some of our past leaders. A succession of politicians left Wales for London with the promise of 'home rule' on their lips. Seduced by London and the trappings of power they failed to deliver. Now for the first time for centuries, we have our own national assembly on the soil of our country. May it grow in power and esteem.

The continuing advance of the Welsh language is a marvel. From the fourteenth century onwards its demise was confidently prophesied. But it still prospers, resilient and supple, the language of both literature and pop culture.

When the Romans occupied Caerleon, 2000 years ago, the children were bilingual in Latin and Welsh. No one foresaw that Welsh would outlive Latin and still be heard in Newport 2000 years later. It is one of a tiny number of minority languages that is guaranteed a continuing life.

The beautiful unique sounds of Welsh have echoed down the centuries. They are still alive and vibrant in the music of Catatonia. The words of Anuerin Bevan are repeated in the songs of the Manic Street Preachers. With joy and surprise Dafydd Iwan celebrates in song that 'Rydym ni yma o hyd' - 'We are still here'.

Here to honour our past heroes. They were not super beings but women and men such as we are. They did great things but often they were fearful and uncertain, as we are. But they won through and deserve our homage.

A new generation will continue Our-story. The renaissance of the Welsh nation has begun. The greatest days of Welsh history are before us.

Paul Flynn MP (Newport West)

PAUL FLYNN: Labour MP for Newport West since 1987 when he ousted sitting Conservative Member Mark Robinson. Former frontbench spokesperson for Wales and Social Security. Campaigning MP and 1996 Spectator Backbencher of the Year. Newspaper columnist for 30 years and author of the best-selling Commons Knowledge: How to be a Backbencher *published in 1997, and his autobiography* Baglu 'Mlaen *(Staggering Forward) published in Welsh in 1998.*

contents

introduction

This book presents the history of Wales as the story of a small nation's struggle to keep its identity and that of its people to achieve control over their own affairs. Taking this stance will hopefully add a little spice to history, for there is more to history than a bland textbook yarn of facts about who was granted what title or who married whom.

On the other hand, of course, it may be argued that there is equally more to Wales than continuous discontent and political revolt to gain an Assembly or parliament, and it is necessary to look at positive factors here, lest any reader think that the author is trying to present a gloomy image of Wales.

A nation is most readily identified by its culture, and by its contribution to our commun human culture, and Wales has a rich heritage going back to its early Celtic roots. The National Eisteddfod, Wales' traditional cultural festival, with competitions in music, singing and poetry (all proceedings conducted in the Welsh language) has origins that go back to 1171, when The Lord Rhys held the first Eisteddfod at Cardigan. Its present form, however, dates from a nineteenth-century revival, instituted in 1880 to preserve traditional Welsh culture. Many places have their own local eisteddfodau and the town of Llangolen, Clwyd, has an international folk festival which invites artists from all over the world, while the Urdd Gobaith Cymru (Welsh League of Youth) Eisteddfod is Europe's largest youth festival.

Professional arts festivals are held annually at St David's Hall, Cardiff, and at Swansea. Famed for its choral singing (particularly male voice choirs), Wales has a tradition of song which is well established. The Welsh National Opera in Cardiff (formed 1945) has an international reputation while, in the north, Theatre Mold is enjoying success.

Connected to the revival of the National Eisteddfod are the foundings, at the beginning of the twentieth century, of the National Museum of Wales (based in Cardiff but with branches throughout the country) and the National Library of Wales in Aberystwyth. Associated with these institutions is the University of Wales, granted its charter in 1893, before which time Welsh students had to go to England or elsewhere to seek a university education.

In 1872 Aberystwyth College opened (women were admitted from 1884). By the turn of the century it had become the University College of Aberystwyth, then part of the University of Wales. Today the University is a federal institution, consisting of the

University Colleges of Aberystwyth, Cardiff, North Wales (at Bangor), St David's College, Lampeter, and the College of Medicine. In 1992 Wales Polytechnic, Treforest, became the University of Glamorgan.

Sianel Pedwar Cymru (S4C), Wales' fourth television channel, broadcasts most of its peak viewing programmes in Welsh, amounting to around 23 hours a week, encouraging opportunities for Welsh-speaking actors. Cardiff is a centre of production activity in both television and cinema, notably in animation. Some companies, such as Siriol, have established a reputation throughout the world.

The youth of Wales finds a voice in rock and pop bands, many of whom have made their mark on the international scene.

In the field of sport, Wales is particularly associated with rugby union football, regarded as the country's national game, with its National Stadium based at Cardiff Arms Park. But the most widely-played team sport is association football, with three professional League clubs and almost 2,000 amateur clubs.

It is in the redevelopment of industry that Wales' economic future lies, and new industries have emerged such as the 'silicon valleys' in South Wales. The extension of the M4 motorway in South Wales links the industrial towns there, via the Severn Bridge, to London, allowing access for trade, while the north has links with Liverpool. It is hoped that economic developments will continue and that Wales can look forward to prosperity through innovations exercised by the Welsh Assembly.

With the arrival of the Assembly, Wales now has a central political voice on its own soil - its first for centuries - and democratic control over its own future. The referendum which brought about the Assembly was a close-run thing, only the narrowest of majorities voting in favour. But, hopefully, as Wales develops, even those who voted against it may warm to it.

Wales' present and future, then, lies in its own people's hands. But what about the past? How did the Assembly come about? What series of made so many of the people of Wales seek a degree of home rule? To understand this, let us look at the nation's history.

chapter one

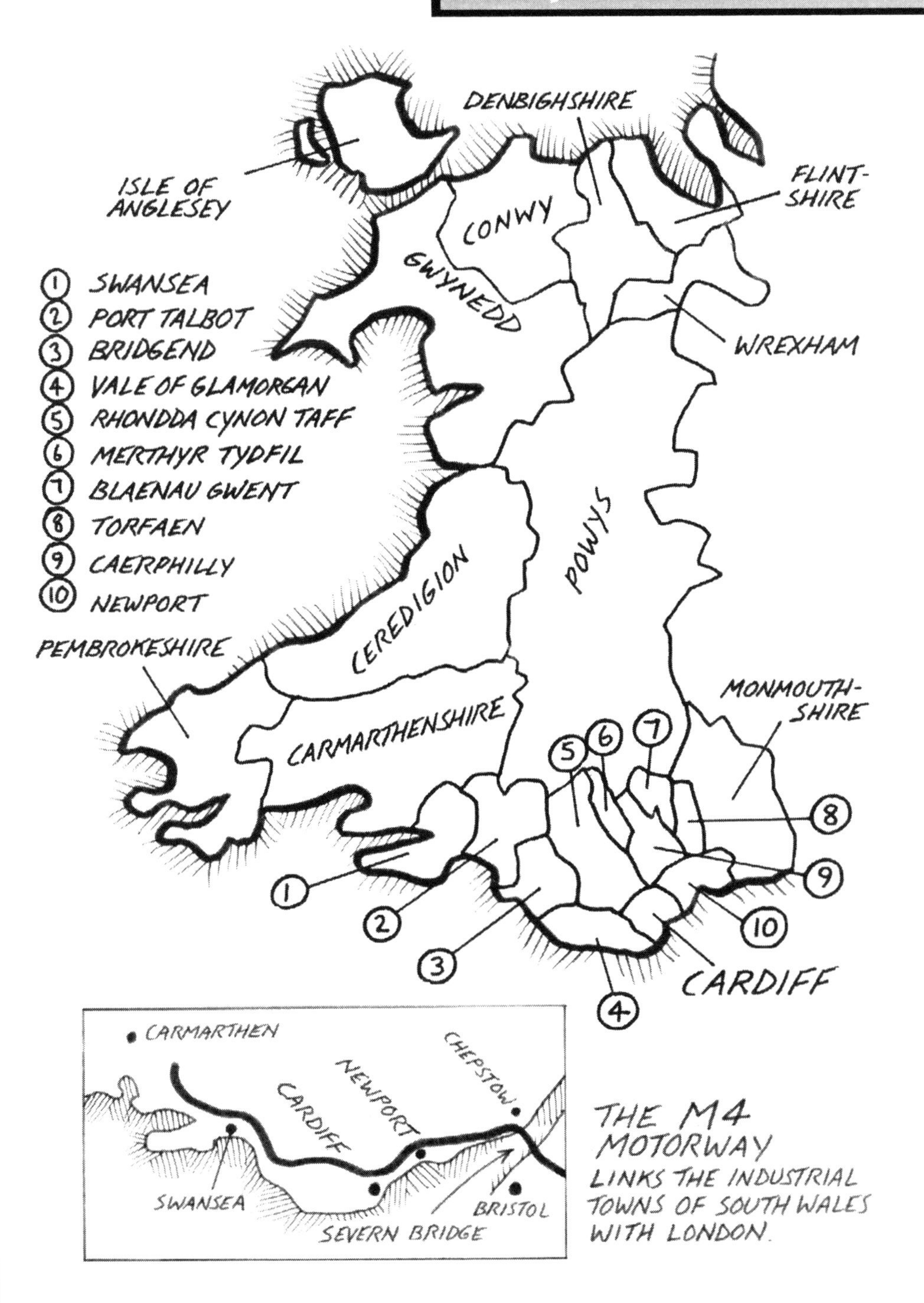
DENBIGHSHIRE
ISLE OF ANGLESEY
FLINTSHIRE
CONWY
GWYNEDD
WREXHAM
1 SWANSEA
2 PORT TALBOT
3 BRIDGEND
4 VALE OF GLAMORGAN
5 RHONDDA CYNON TAFF
6 MERTHYR TYDFIL
7 BLAENAU GWENT
8 TORFAEN
9 CAERPHILLY
10 NEWPORT
POWYS
CEREDIGION
PEMBROKESHIRE
MONMOUTHSHIRE
CARMARTHENSHIRE
CARDIFF
CARMARTHEN
CHEPSTOW
NEWPORT
CARDIFF
SWANSEA
BRISTOL
SEVERN BRIDGE
THE M4 MOTORWAY
LINKS THE INDUSTRIAL TOWNS OF SOUTH WALES WITH LONDON.

THE LAND WE NOW CALL WALES ONCE FORMED THE BED OF A TRILOBITE-INFESTED SEA, AROUND 550 MILLION YEARS AGO. THE ROCKS DATING FROM THIS PERIOD ARE CLASSED AS CAMBRIAN, FROM THE ROMAN NAME FOR WALES.

THIS TERRAIN HAS AFFECTED WALES' HISTORY, OFFERING REFUGE AND ISOLATION TO ITS PEOPLE WHEN UNDER ATTACK OR INVASION, BUT ALSO MAKING COMMUNICATION DIFFICULT. IT HAS MADE COMMUNITIES CLOSELY-KNIT, BUT IT HAS ALSO CREATED AN OBSTACLE TO UNIFICATION.
THE ISOLATION OF COMMUNITIES HAS HELPED TO PRESERVE WELSH LANGUAGE AND TRADITIONS UNTIL RELATIVELY RECENTLY.

THE RUGGED WELSH LANDSCAPE WAS CARVED BY THE MOVEMENT OF GLACIERS THROUGHOUT THE LAST ICE AGE (c.70,000-10,000 BC), DURING WHICH THERE WERE WARMER INTERGLACIAL PERIODS WHEN STONE-AGE PEOPLE LIVED IN WALES. THESE HUNTERS CHASED THE HERDS OF GAME THAT LIVED ON THE TUNDRA WHICH COVERED THE LAND AS THE GLACIERS RETREATED NORTHWARDS.

EARLY REMAINS OF CRO-MAGNON MAN FOUND AT GOAT'S HOLE CAVE, PAVILAND, REVEALED THE SKELETON OF A YOUNG MAN WITH A NECKLACE MADE OF TEETH OF MAMMOTH, WOOLLY RHINOCEROS AND HYENA. THESE STONE AGE HUNTERS REMAINED FEW IN NUMBER, CROSSING TO SOUTHERN BRITAIN FROM CONTINENTAL EUROPE WHEN MAINLAND BRITAIN WAS JOINED BY LAND TO THE CONTINENT BEFORE THE MELTING OF THE ICE SHEETS RAISED THE SEA LEVEL.

AROUND 6000 BC, NEOLITHIC FARMING COMMUNITIES ARRIVED, SETTLING PERMANENTLY IN WESTERN PARTS OF THE BRITISH ISLES. FROM THE MEDITERRANEAN AREA, THE SMALL, DARK-HAIRED PEOPLE CROSSED THE ENGLISH CHANNEL IN PRIMITIVE BOATS. USING STONE TOOLS, THEY CLEARED AREAS OF THE FOREST WHICH THEN COVERED THE LAND AND RAISED BARLEY, WHEAT, RYE, SHEEP AND CATTLE. AS THEY BECAME MORE SETTLED AND PROSPEROUS, AND THEIR SOCIETY MORE ORGANISED, THE CEREMONIAL BURIAL OF THEIR DEAD - ESPECIALLY OF IMPORTANT LEADERS - INVOLVED LAYING THE BODY UNDER A STONE TABLE OR 'CROMLECH'. IN TIME, THESE TOMBS BECAME MORE ELABORATE, OFTEN TAKING THE FORM OF AN EARTH MOUND OR MAN-MADE HILL CALLED A 'BARROW'.

THIS 'MEGALITHIC' (GIANT STONE) CULTURE BECAME MORE PRONOUNCED WITH THE ARRIVAL OF THE 'BEAKER PEOPLE' FROM THE IBERIAN PENINSULA DURING THE 2ND MILLENNIUM B.C. SETTLING MAINLY IN EASTERN PARTS OF BRITAIN, SOME SETTLED IN SOUTH WALES, GETTING THEIR NAME FROM THEIR PRACTICE OF BURYING EARTHENWARE BEAKERS ALONG WITH THEIR DEAD. THEY BUILT THE GREAT STONE CIRCLES OR HENGES OF ANCIENT BRITAIN, AND INDEED THE INNER CIRCLE OF BLUE STONES OF STONEHENGE CAME FROM THE PRESELI HILLS OF PEMBROKESHIRE, WALES, AROUND 2000 BC.

THE STONE CIRCLES WERE SOLAR TEMPLES, CENTRES OF RELIGIOUS CEREMONY AND RITUAL MAGIC (IN OCCULT LORE, IT IS BELIEVED THEY HARNESS LIFE-GIVING 'EARTH ENERGY'). THEY WERE ALSO USED FOR MEASURING THE POSITION OF THE SUN, FORMING A MEANS OF CALCULATING A CALENDAR - IMPORTANT TO AN AGRICULTURAL SOCIETY FOR PLANNING THE GROWING OF CROPS.

FEW WEAPONS AND EVIDENCE OF FORTRESSES FROM THIS PERIOD HAVE BEEN FOUND, SUGGESTING THAT THESE PEOPLE WERE MAINLY UNWARLIKE, BUT TRADING IN TOOLS AND UTENSILS WAS ESTABLISHED ALONG THE SEA ROUTE BETWEEN THE WESTERN PARTS OF THE BRITISH ISLES AND THE IBERIAN PENINSULA.

EVENTUALLY, STONE GAVE WAY TO METAL AS THE MAIN MATERIAL USED FOR MAKING TOOLS AND WEAPONS, FIRST WITH THE BRONZE AGE (c.2000-500 BC, WHEN THE CELTS ARRIVED), AND THEN TO THE IRON AGE (500 BC - AD 80, WITH THE ARRIVAL OF THE ROMANS).

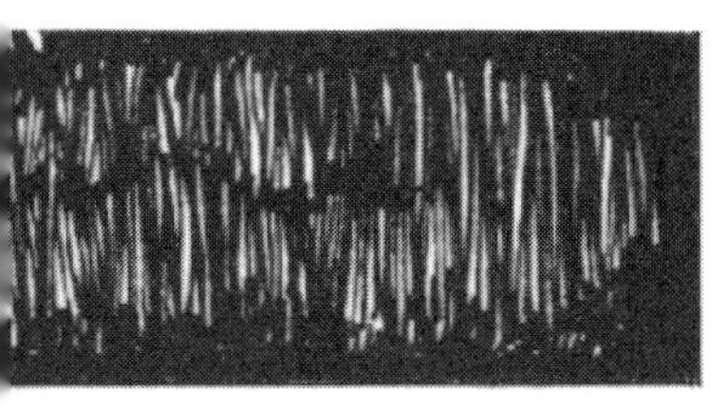

WHO WERE THE CELTS?
THE PEOPLE WHO GAVE WALES ITS IDENTITY AND CULTURE, THAT'S WHO!

CELTIC BRITAIN TRADED WITH THE ROMAN EMPIRE, EXCHANGING GRAIN, METALS AND (LESS PLEASANTLY) SLAVES FOR LUXURY GOODS.
BUT IN AD 43 THE ROMAN EMPEROR CLAUDIUS, EAGER TO WIN THE SUPPORT OF THE ARMY (WHO INSTALLED HIM IN POWER) AND THE SENATE, DECIDED TO LAUNCH AN INVASION OF BRITAIN.

THE CELTS, ORIGINALLY FROM CENTRAL EUROPE (THEIR NAME COMES FROM THE GREEK WORD FOR THEM: KELTOI), WERE A VERY WARLIKE PEOPLE BUT, AS WE SHALL SEE, IT WAS THEY WHO SHAPED THE WELSH NATION. THEY LIVED IN KINSHIP GROUPS OR CLANS WHICH FORMED PARTS OF LARGER TRIBES AND HAD A SPLENDID CULTURE. CELTIC ART AND DESIGN, WHICH CAN BE FOUND IN EVERYTHING FROM TOOLS TO JEWELLERY, UTENSILS TO CLOTHING, USED A UNIQUE PATTERN OF STYLISED ANIMALS, INTERWOVEN LATTICEWORK AND SWIRLING OR SPIRALLING LINES.

RHIANNON, HORSE GODDESS OF THE WELSH CELTS.

THE RELIGION OF THE EARLY CELTS WAS PAGAN. THEY WORSHIPPED NATURE DEITIES SUCH AS CERNUNNOS, THE HORNED GOD OF FERTILITY; DIANA, GODDESS OF THE MOON AND HUNTING; AND CERIDWEN, GODDESS OF MAGIC AND WISDOM. HUMAN SACRIFICE MAY HAVE BEEN INCLUDED IN THEIR RITUALS, AS SOME ROMAN ACCOUNTS RELATE.

THE MEETING PLACES OF THE DRUIDS WERE SACRED GROVES. IN WALES, DRUID ACTIVITY WAS CENTRED IN THE SACRED GROVES OF ANGLESEY, LATER DESTROYED BY THE ROMANS, WHO PUT AN END TO THE PRACTICES OF THE DRUIDS.

THE ROMANS FOUND THE TRIBES OF CAMBRIA (CYMRU OR WALES) PARTICULARLY DIFFICULT TO CONQUER AND SUBDUE. UNDER THEIR CHIEF, CARADOG (CARACTACUS), THE CAMBRIAN TRIBES LED A FIERCE RESISTANCE ALONG THE WELSH BORDER UNTIL, IN AD 51, CARADOG WAS DEFEATED IN BATTLE IN THE SEVERN VALLEY. HE SOUGHT REFUGE AMONG THE BRIGANTES, IN THE NORTH OF WHAT IS NOW ENGLAND, BUT THEIR QUEEN, CARTIMANDUA, TURNED HIM OVER TO THE ROMANS. TAKEN BEFORE CLAUDIUS HIMSELF, CARADOG PUT UP SUCH A SHOW OF PROUD DEFIANCE THAT CLAUDIUS RELEASED HIM IN TRIBUTE TO HIS COURAGE. CARADOG DIED IN ROME AROUND AD 54.

BUT EVEN AFTER THE DEFEAT OF CARADOG, IT TOOK THE ROMANS OVER 20 YEARS OF FURTHER FIGHTING TO SUPPRESS THE TRIBES IN WALES.
THE ROMANS INTRODUCED FINE BUILDINGS AND ROADS AS WELL AS ENSLAVEMENT AND TAXATION. THOUGH NATIVE CELTS COULD BE TAKEN AS SLAVES, THEY COULD ALSO CHOOSE TO JOIN THE ROMAN ARMY. THE ROMAN LEGIONS WERE MULTINATIONAL, COMPRISING MEN FROM DIFFERENT PROVINCES OF THE EMPIRE.

ALTHOUGH THE ROMANS HAD ABOLISHED THE DRUIDS, THEY DID NOT OBJECT TO LOCAL GODS BEING WORSHIPPED. THE ROMANS' OWN DEITIES INCLUDED JUPITER, THEIR CHIEF GOD; VENUS, GODDESS OF LOVE; MARS, GOD OF WAR, etc. CERTAIN EMPERORS, SUCH AS CLAUDIUS, WERE ALSO WORSHIPPED AS GODS IN HUMAN INCARNATION.

CALL ME GOD

THEN, AFTER THE EMPEROR CONSTANTINE BECAME CHRISTIAN IN AD 312, CHRISTIANITY BECAME THE OFFICIAL RELIGION OF THE STATE AND THE EMPIRE, AND WAS INTRODUCED TO THE CELTIC TRIBES IN BRITAIN. IT TOOK ROOT IN WALES, PARTICULARLY IN THE SOUTH EAST, REMAINING EVEN AFTER THE ROMANS LEFT.

CLAVDIVS

IN THE 4th CENTURY AD BEGAN THE DECLINE OF THE ROMAN EMPIRE. PRESSED FROM OUTSIDE BY INVASIONS OF BARBARIAN TRIBES (GOTHS, VANDALS, HUNS) AND FROM INSIDE BY DISUNITY AND CORRUPTION, THE EMPIRE BEGAN TO COLLAPSE. ROMAN ARMIES WERE WITHDRAWN FROM BRITAIN IN AD 407. DESPITE BRIEF PARTIAL REOCCUPATIONS, ROMAN OCCUPATION ENDED AFTER c. AD 450.

THE BRITISH ISLES, LIKE THE REST OF EUROPE, THEN ENTERED THE **DARK AGES**, WHEN THE EUROPEAN PEOPLES FORMED THEMSELVES INTO A MULTITUDE OF TINY KINGDOMS FIGHTING EACH OTHER FOR SURVIVAL, CONTROL OR TERRITORY. WEAKER TRIBES, FORMERLY DEPENDENT ON THE 'PROTECTION' OF ROMAN TROOPS, BECAME EXPOSED TO CONQUEST BY STRONGER ONES, WHO IN TURN WOULD BE SUBDUED BY STILL STRONGER NATIONS. THE DARK AGES (5th-10th CENTURIES A.D.) GET THEIR NAME FROM THE INTELLECTUAL 'DARKNESS' OF THE PERIOD, LACKING THE ENLIGHTENMENT OF SCIENTIFIC KNOWLEDGE, ART OR LITERATURE.

EUROPE, DIVIDED INTO SO MANY SMALL, WARRING UNITS, LACKED THE CIVIL PEACE OR POLITICAL STABILITY NEEDED FOR THE ORGANISATION OF LARGE SCHOOLS AND UNIVERSITIES. MAINLY MONKS WERE LITERATE, PRESERVING, COPYING AND ILLUSTRATING SACRED OR CLASSICAL TEXTS FOR FUTURE GENERATIONS.

AS ROMAN RULE ENDED, THE PERIOD AROUND A.D. 400-600 MARKS AN IMPORTANT EPOCH IN WELSH HISTORY AS MUCH OF BRITAIN FELL TO THE ANGLO-SAXONS, GERMANIC INVADERS FROM SCHLESWIG-HOLSTEIN, THE PENINSULA BETWEEN WHAT IS NOW DENMARK AND GERMANY. FORMING TWO GROUPS, THE ANGLES SETTLED MAINLY IN NORTHERN AND EASTERN ENGLAND, THE SAXONS IN SOUTHERN ENGLAND. THEIR CONQUEST OF ENGLAND OVER THIS PERIOD WAS GRADUAL, INTERMARRYING WITH THE NATIVE BRITONS.

SO BRITAIN BECAME DIVIDED INTO THE BRYTHONIC WEST, TEUTONIC EAST AND GAELIC NORTH, COMING TO FORM THE NATIONS OF WALES, ENGLAND AND SCOTLAND RESPECTIVELY. WALES BECAME MORE DISTINCT, ITS IDENTITY AND LANGUAGE REFINED AND ITS BORDERS RECOGNISABLE.

AND SO, OUT OF THE TURMOIL OF THE DARK AGES, THE NATION OF WALES WAS BORN!

THE CELTIC CHURCH WAS A UNIFYING FACTOR IN WALES. ALREADY PARTLY CHRISTIANISED BY THE ROMANS, THE WELSH CELTS READILY ADOPTED CELTIC CHRISTIANITY.

INDEED, WALES BECAME DEFENSIVELY CHRISTIAN WHILE THE ANGLO-SAXONS WERE STILL PAGAN (BEFORE ST. AUGUSTINE CONVERTED THEM IN 597). SURVIVING CHRONICLES OF DARK AGE WALES TELL OF CONTEMPORARY MONKS AND SAINTS.

FOREMOST AMONG THOSE SAINTS WAS ST. DAVID OR DEWI (d. 589), WHO FOUNDED A MONASTERY AT GLYN RHOSYN AROUND AD 530. HE TAUGHT THAT INNER PEACE AND HAPPINESS ARE TO BE FOUND THROUGH SELF-CONTROL, AVOIDING WORLDLY POSSESSIONS AND PLEASURES. DESPITE THE HARSHNESS OF THIS SELF-DISCIPLINE, DEWI SANT ATTRACTED A HUGE FOLLOWING, AND MANY LEGENDS WERE LATER ATTACHED TO HIM, CREDITING HIM WITH SUPERNATURAL POWERS AND CLAIMING HIM TO BE UNCLE OF KING ARTHUR.
THEY SAY HE CAN WORK MIRACLE CURES!
HUH! I'M NOT HERE TO DO MAGIC TRICKS!
I'VE HEARD HE CAN MAKE WELLS APPEAR!
THE GROUND CAN RISE BENEATH HIS FEET!

ANCIENT WALES IS STEEPED IN LEGEND, WITH MANY TALES OF MAGIC, OF CELTIC MYTHOLOGY AND OF THE SUPERNATURAL FEATURING LARGELY IN WELSH LITERATURE, NOTABLY THE 14th CENTURY 'MABINOGION' (TALES FROM THE WHITE BOOK OF RHYDDERCH) IN WHICH HEROES AND HEROINES OF INDEPENDENT WALES PURSUE ADVENTURES IN ROMANCE AND CHIVALRY AGAINST A BACKDROP OF MAGIC AND FOLKLORE, INSPIRING FANTASY WRITING TO THE PRESENT DAY.

THE MOST UNIFYING FACTOR OF ALL, HOWEVER, WAS DEFENCE AGAINST SAXON ATTACK.
MYRDDIN
MERLIN
IN THE 6th CENTURY, CELTIC LEADER ARTHUR ('KING ARTHUR' OF LEGEND) APPEARS TO HAVE LED AN ANTI-SAXON REBELLION. THE ADOPTION OF Y DDRAIG GOCH (THE RED DRAGON) AS THE SYMBOL OF WALES DATES FROM THIS PERIOD.
LET'S TAKE A QUICK LOOK AT THE LEGENDS...

ACCORDING TO POPULAR FOLKLORE, KING ARTHUR WAS BORN IN TINTAGEL CASTLE, CORNWALL, ORPHANED SON OF KING UTHER PENDRAGON. WHEN HE GREW UP TO BE KING, THE LEGENDARY ARTHUR CONFERRED WITH HIS KNIGHTS AROUND A ROUND TABLE SO THAT THEY COULD NOT SQUABBLE OVER RANK, AS WOULD NORMALLY BE ESTABLISHED BY THE SEATING ARRANGEMENTS AT A KING'S TABLE.

IN FACT, LITTLE IS KNOWN OF THE REAL ARTHUR (ARDDYR), WHO LED THE CELTS AGAINST THE SAXONS, LED BY VORTIGERN, WHOM THEY DEFEATED AT THE BATTLE OF MOUNT BADON c. AD 520. RATHER THAN KING, ARTHUR WAS PROBABLY COMMANDER-IN-CHIEF OF ALL THE COMBINED CELTIC FORCES AGAINST THE SAXONS. HIS WELSH WIZARD AND ADVISOR MYRDDIN (MERLIN) IS SAID TO BE BURIED IN A CAVE AT DINEFWR CASTLE, DYFED. ARTHUR HIMSELF, ACCORDING TO LEGEND, IS SAID TO BE LAID TO REST IN THE CAVE OF CRAIG Y DDINAS, NEAR GLYNNEDD, GLAMORGAN.

IN ANOTHER VERSION, MERLIN WAS ASKED BY A LORD OF A WELSH CASTLE TO SOLVE A CURSE OVER (OR, RATHER, UNDER) THE CASTLE. HE DISCOVERED AND RELEASED THE TWO DRAGONS UNDER THE CASTLE, WHO THEN FOUGHT, THE RED ONE DEFEATING THE WHITE ONE BEFORE FLYING OFF. SINCE THE WELSH FOUGHT OFF THE SAXONS, SUCCESSFULLY DEFENDING WALES AGAINST INVASION, THE RED DRAGON IN THE LEGEND BECAME USED AS THE SYMBOL OF WELSH NATIONHOOD.

chapter two

WALES, LIKE THE REST OF BRITAIN AND OTHER EUROPEAN COUNTRIES AT THIS TIME, WAS DIVIDED INTO A NUMBER OF TINY KINGDOMS (SEE MAPS ON NEXT PAGE), THOUGH SHARING A COMMON WELSH LANGUAGE AND CULTURE. THE STRONGEST OF THESE IN THE EARLY/MID 6th CENTURY WAS GWYNEDD, RULED BY MAELGWN (d. AD 547). IN THE SOUTH WEST, THE KINGDOM OF DYFED WAS ALSO STRONG, RULED BY KING VORTIPOR. ECCLESIASTICAL SCHOLAR GILDAS, WHO RECORDED EVENTS AT THE TIME, DESCRIBES THESE TWO MEN AS 'SINFUL', INDULGING IN TOO MUCH DRINKING AND MUSIC, BUT THIS IGNORED THEIR STRENGTHS. IN AN AGE OF BARBARISM, THESE TWO MANAGED TO KEEP CIVIL ORDER, AND WERE PATRONS OF THE ARTS AS WELL. THE WELSH CALLED THEMSELVES CYMRY, MEANING COMRADES OR COUNTRYMEN. THEY REGARDED OTHER CELTIC BRITONS AS CYMRY ALSO BUT, AFTER SAXON KING AETHELFRITH DEFEATED THE WELSH AT CHESTER IN AD 613, IT WAS OBVIOUS THAT THE CYMRY WOULD BE CONFINED TO WALES, CUT OFF FROM THEIR CELTIC ALLIES TO THE NORTH.

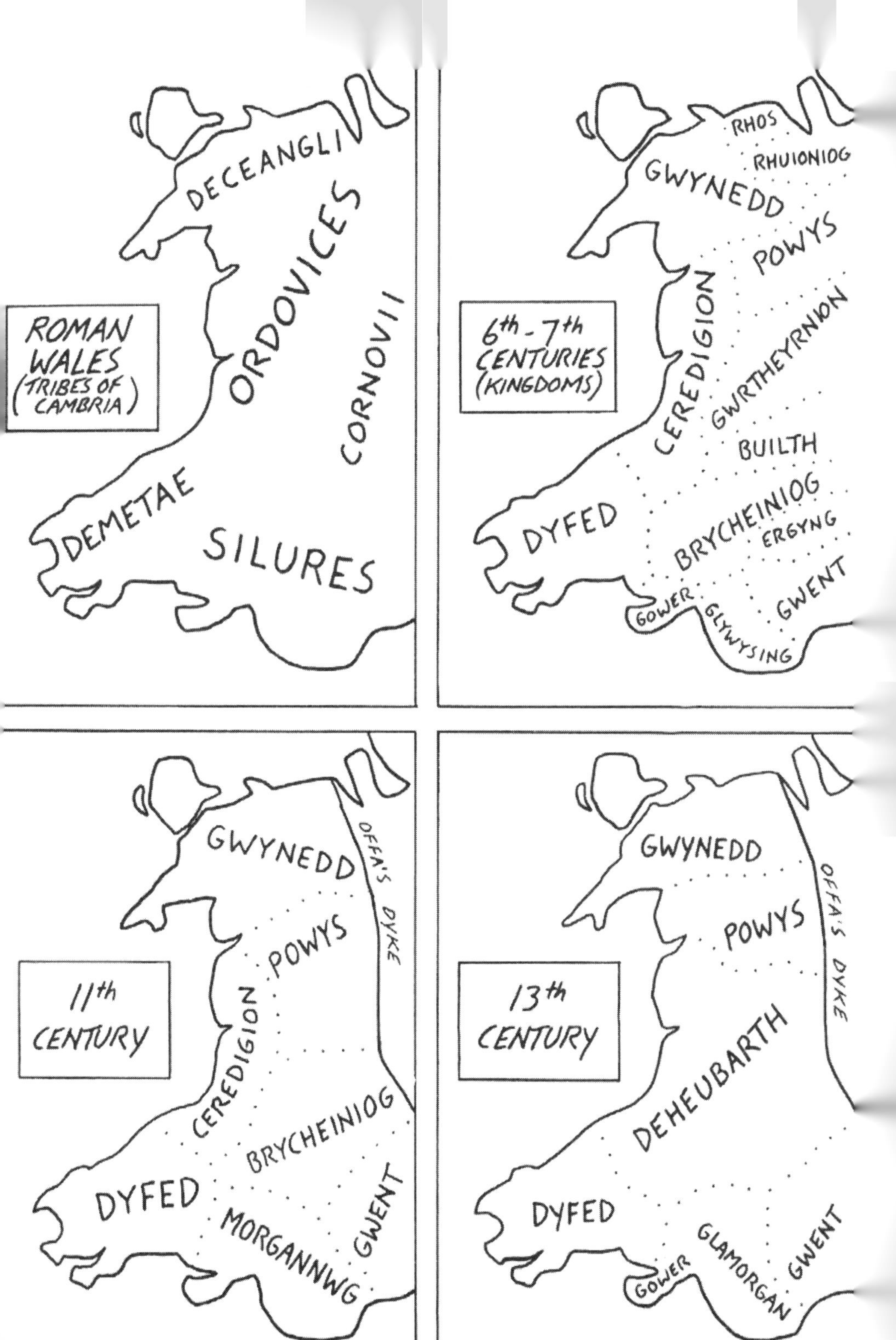
ROMAN WALES (TRIBES OF CAMBRIA)
DECEANGLI
ORDOVICES
CORNOVII
DEMETAE
SILURES
6th - 7th CENTURIES (KINGDOMS)
RHOS
RHUIONIOG
GWYNEDD
POWYS
CEREDIGION
GWRTHEYRNION
BUILTH
DYFED
BRYCHEINIOG
ERGYNG
GWENT
GOWER
GLYWYSING
11th CENTURY
GWYNEDD
OFFA'S DYKE
POWYS
CEREDIGION
BRYCHEINIOG
DYFED
MORGANNWG
GWENT
13th CENTURY
GWYNEDD
POWYS
OFFA'S DYKE
DEHEUBARTH
DYFED
GLAMORGAN
GWENT
GOWER

AFTER AETHELFRITH'S DEATH, CADWALLON, SON OF THE RENOWNED KING CADFAN OF GWYNEDD, DECIDED THAT THE BEST WAY TO RESTORE CELTIC POWER WAS TO LAUNCH AN ATTACK ON NORTHUMBRIA, IN THE NORTH OF ENGLAND, AIDING THE BRITONS THERE, RATHER THAN ON NEIGHBOURING MERCIA, IN THE ENGLISH MIDLANDS. HE FORMED AN ALLIANCE WITH PENDA, KING OF MERCIA, AND WENT TO WAR AGAINST KING OSWALD OF NORTHUMBRIA, BUT DIED IN BATTLE AT HEAVENFIELD (AD 634), NEAR HADRIAN'S WALL. LATER, AT THE BATTLE OF MASERFIELD (AD 642), PENDA KILLED OSWALD. MERCIA AND WESSEX (SOUTHERN ENGLAND) NOW LOOKED TOWARDS EACH OTHER AS THE NEXT ACQUISITION IN UNITING ALL OF ENGLAND. AROUND AD 770, MERCIA'S KING OFFA CONSTRUCTED **OFFA'S DYKE**, A BARRIER SEPARATING ENGLAND FROM THE 'WEALAS' (FOREIGNERS), FROM WHICH WALES GETS ITS ENGLISH NAME. OFFA'S DYKE FORMED A FORMAL BORDER BETWEEN WALES AND ENGLAND. IT WAS NOT INTENDED TO BE AN IMPENETRABLE WALL, RATHER AN AGREED FRONTIER TO REMIND BOTH SIDES WHERE THEIR TERRITORIES MET, THOUGH IT WOULD BE AN OBSTACLE TO RAIDING PARTIES.

WITH A PEACE WITH MERCIA SECURED, AND THE SAXONS LESS OF A THREAT, VIKING RAIDERS INSTEAD BECAME A MENACE IN THE 9th CENTURY, PARTICULARLY AFTER THE VIKINGS ESTABLISHED COLONIES IN IRELAND AND THE ISLE OF MAN, UNTIL RHODRI FAWR (OR 'MAWR', i.e. RHODRI THE GREAT), KING OF GWYNEDD, KILLED VIKING CHIEF HORN IN BATTLE IN ANGLESEY IN A.D. 856. THROUGH MARRIAGE, DIPLOMACY AND MILITARY STRENGTH, RHODRI FAWR BECAME THE FIRST WELSH KING TO UNITE MOST OF WALES AND BRING IT UNDER HIS CONTROL.

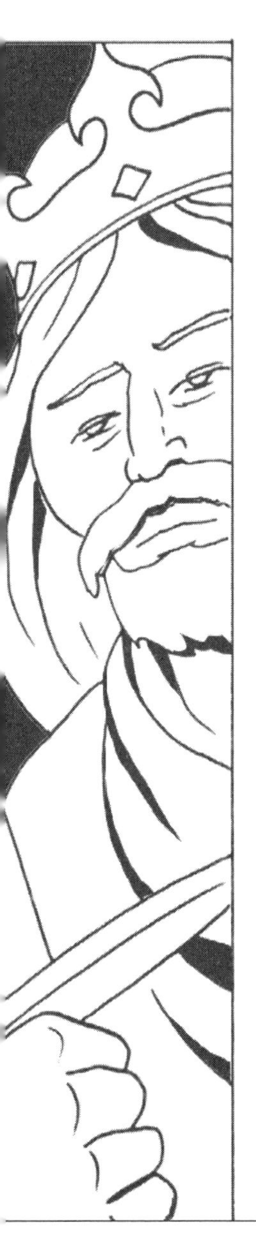

ENGLAND, TOO, BECAME UNITED UNDER EDWARD THE ELDER, BUT BORDER WARFARE CONTINUED AND RHODRI DIED IN BATTLE IN 878. AFTER HIS DEATH, HIS KINGDOM WAS DIVIDED AMONG HIS SONS. THE LESSER WELSH STATES TURNED FOR PROTECTION TO ALFRED THE GREAT, KING OF ENGLAND, BUT WHEN HE DIED IN 901, WALES FELL INTO CONFUSION AND STRIFE UNTIL HYWEL DDA (HOWELL THE GOOD), GRANDSON OF RHODRI FAWR, SUCCEEDED IN REUNITING THE COUNTRY. HAVING MARRIED ELEN, DAUGHTER OF THE KING OF DYFED, LLYWARCH AP HAFAIDD, HIS RULE OVER SOUTHERN WALES WAS ASSURED.

HE THEN WENT ON TO CONQUER THE NORTHERN KINGDOMS OF GWYNEDD AND POWYS IN 942. HYWEL INTRODUCED MINTED CURRENCY AND A UNIFYING CODE OF LAW. HIS DEATH IN 950 PUT WALES INTO DISARRAY AGAIN AND THE COUNTRY WAS HARASSED BY DANISH ATTACKS THROUGHOUT THE 10th CENTURY (THOUGH AT LEAST THE DANES DID NOT CONQUER AND SETTLE IN WALES AS THEY DID IN ENGLAND UNDER CNUT).

ALES BECAME UNIFIED AGAIN UNDER GRUFFUDD AP LLYWELYN, SON OF THE DEPOSED KING OF GWYNEDD, LLYWELYN AP SEISYLLT.

ACCORDING TO A STORY WRITTEN A CENTURY AFTER HIS TIME, YOUNG GRUFFUD, A LAZY YOUTH, WAS OUT WALKING ONE NIGHT WHEN HE OVERHEARD A FAMILY IN A HOUSE COOKING STEW FOR DINNER...

HAVING GAINED CONTROL OF GWYNEDD AND POWYS, GRUFFUDD DEFEATED AN ENGLISH ARMY AT THE BATTLE OF RHYD-Y-GROES (1039) AND THEN WENT ON, THAT SAME YEAR, TO SEIZE CONTROL OF THE OTHER WELSH TERRITORIES, BECOMING THE FIRST KING OF THE WHOLE OF WALES. GRUFFUDD MADE PEACE WITH ENGLAND'S EDWARD THE CONFESSOR. HOWEVER HAROLD, EARL OF MERCIA, PERSUADED EDWARD TO LET HIM TRY A NEW ATTACK ON WALES IN THE WINTER OF 1062-63. HAROLD UNEXPECTEDLY ATTACKED FROM THE WEST, HAVING SAILED AROUND THE COAST OF WALES FROM THE BRISTOL CHANNEL. SUPPORT FOR GRUFFUDD FELL AWAY AS HIS FOLLOWERS SAW THE FUTILITY OF RESISTANCE AGAINST THE ONCOMING ATTACK AND, IN AUGUST 1063, GRUFFUDD WAS BETRAYED AND KILLED BY HIS OWN MEN. (THREE YEARS LATER, AS KING OF ENGLAND, HAROLD DIED AT HASTINGS).

SO, ALTHOUGH SUCH WELSH KINGS AS RHODRI FAWR, HYWEL DDA AND GRUFFUDD AP LLYWELYN UNITED THE COUNTRY TEMPORARILY, WALES SPENT MOST OF THE DARK AGES DIVIDED INTO SMALLER KINGDOMS.

chapter three

THESE NORMAN CASTLES, RUINS TODAY BUT STILL BEAUTIFUL AND IMPRESSIVE, ARE AN IMPORTANT PART OF WALES' HERITAGE. THE POWERFUL NORMANS WHO BUILT THEM WERE THE 'LORDS MARCHER', LOCALISED OVERLORDS WHO WERE ABLE TO LIVE OUTSIDE THE LAW OF THE KING OF ENGLAND BUT ENFORCE THEIR OWN LAWS OVER THE NATIVE WELSH, WHOM THEY COULD RECRUIT INTO MILITARY SERVICE. 'STRONGBOW' (RICHARD DE CLARE, EARL OF PEMBROKE) LED A COMBINED ARMY OF NORMANS AND WELSH INTO IRELAND, FOR EXAMPLE, IN 1170.

NORMAN INFLUENCE WAS NOT UNSHAKEABLE. FIGURES LIKE OWAIN GWYNEDD AND RHYS AP GRUFFUDD LED NATIVE RESISTANCE, ENSURING THE SURVIVAL OF WELSH PRINCIPALITIES
EVEN IF SURROUNDED BY ANGLO-NORMAN LORDSHIPS.
AND WELSH CULTURE AND IDENTITY CONTINUED TO THRIVE.

THE HINTERLAND OF WALES, BEYOND THE SOUTHERN AND EASTERN FRINGES UNDER ANGLO-NORMAN OCCUPATION, WAS KNOWN AS 'PURA WALIA'.

HERE, THE WELSH KINGS OR PRINCES HELD OUT, SUCH AS RHYS AP TEWDWR, KING OF DEHEUBARTH. HIS DEATH IN 1093 WAS SEEN AS AN END OF INDEPENDENT KINGSHIP IN WALES AT THE TIME, AS WELSH RULERS OR PRINCES THEREAFTER PAID HOMAGE TO THE KING OF ENGLAND.

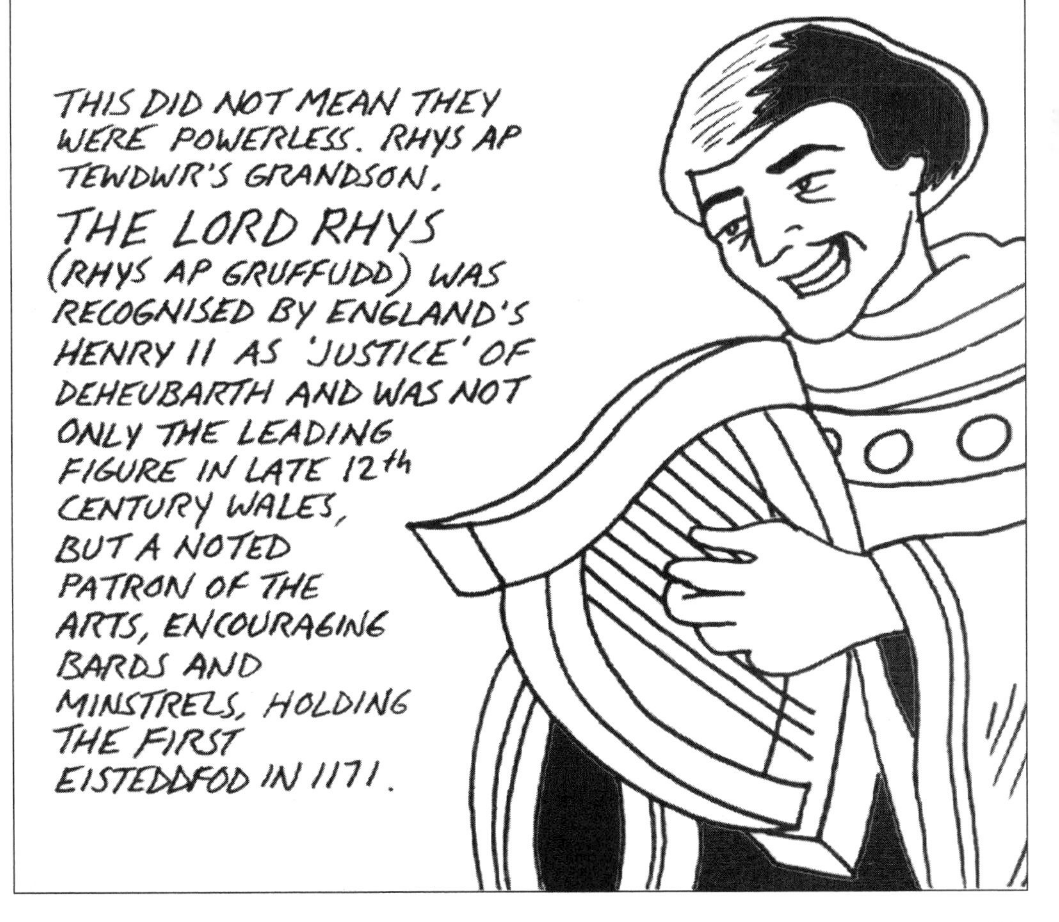

THIS DID NOT MEAN THEY WERE POWERLESS. RHYS AP TEWDWR'S GRANDSON,

THE LORD RHYS

(RHYS AP GRUFFUDD) WAS RECOGNISED BY ENGLAND'S HENRY II AS 'JUSTICE' OF DEHEUBARTH AND WAS NOT ONLY THE LEADING FIGURE IN LATE 12th CENTURY WALES, BUT A NOTED PATRON OF THE ARTS, ENCOURAGING BARDS AND MINSTRELS, HOLDING THE FIRST EISTEDDFOD IN 1171.

IN 1188 THE SCHOLAR GIRALDUS CAMBRENSIS (GERALD THE WELSHMAN) ACCOMPANIED ARCHBISHOP BALDWIN THROUGH WALES TO PREACH THE THIRD CRUSADE. IN HIS 'DESCRIPTION OF WALES' HE IMAGINES A CONVERSATION BETWEEN ENGLAND'S HENRY II AND AN OLD WELSHMAN.

ERALD WAS BORN c. 1146 AT MANORBIER CASTLE, PEMBROKESHIRE. THOUGH HE FAILED IN HIS AMBITION TO GAIN AUTONOMY FOR THE CHURCH IN WALES THROUGH AN ARCHBISHOPRIC OF ST DAVID'S, MAKING IT INDEPENDENT OF CANTERBURY, HE WAS A GIFTED SCHOLAR AND WRITER.

WRITTEN AROUND 1194, 'DESCRIPTION OF WALES', TOGETHER WITH GERALD'S OTHER FAMOUS BOOK 'ITINERARY THROUGH WALES', WRITTEN ABOUT 3 YEARS EARLIER, GIVE LIVELY ANECDOTAL ACCOUNTS AND DESCRIPTIONS OF WELSH LIFE WHICH HAVE BEEN AN IMPORTANT SOURCE OF INFORMATION TO LATER HISTORIANS.

'DESCRIPTION OF WALES' NOTES THE MARKED INCREASE IN POPULATION IN THE 12th AND 13th CENTURIES, BOTH NATIVE AND FROM IMMIGRATION FROM ENGLAND.

IT GIVES DETAILS OF HOW MOST WELSH PEOPLE LIVED: THEY DWELT IN WICKERWORK HOVELS AND SLEPT ON RUSHES BUT ENTERTAINED VISITORS WITH MUSIC ON THE HARP. FOOD WAS NOT PLENTIFUL, BUT THEY ATE A HEALTHY DIET OF MEAT, OATS AND DAIRY PRODUCTS. THEY CLEANED THEIR TEETH WITH TWIGS, AND BOTH SEXES WORE PUDDING-BOWL HAIRCUTS. THE POPULATION WAS SCATTERED: THE WELSH (BEYOND THE NORMAN CASTLES) DID NOT LIVE IN TOWNS.

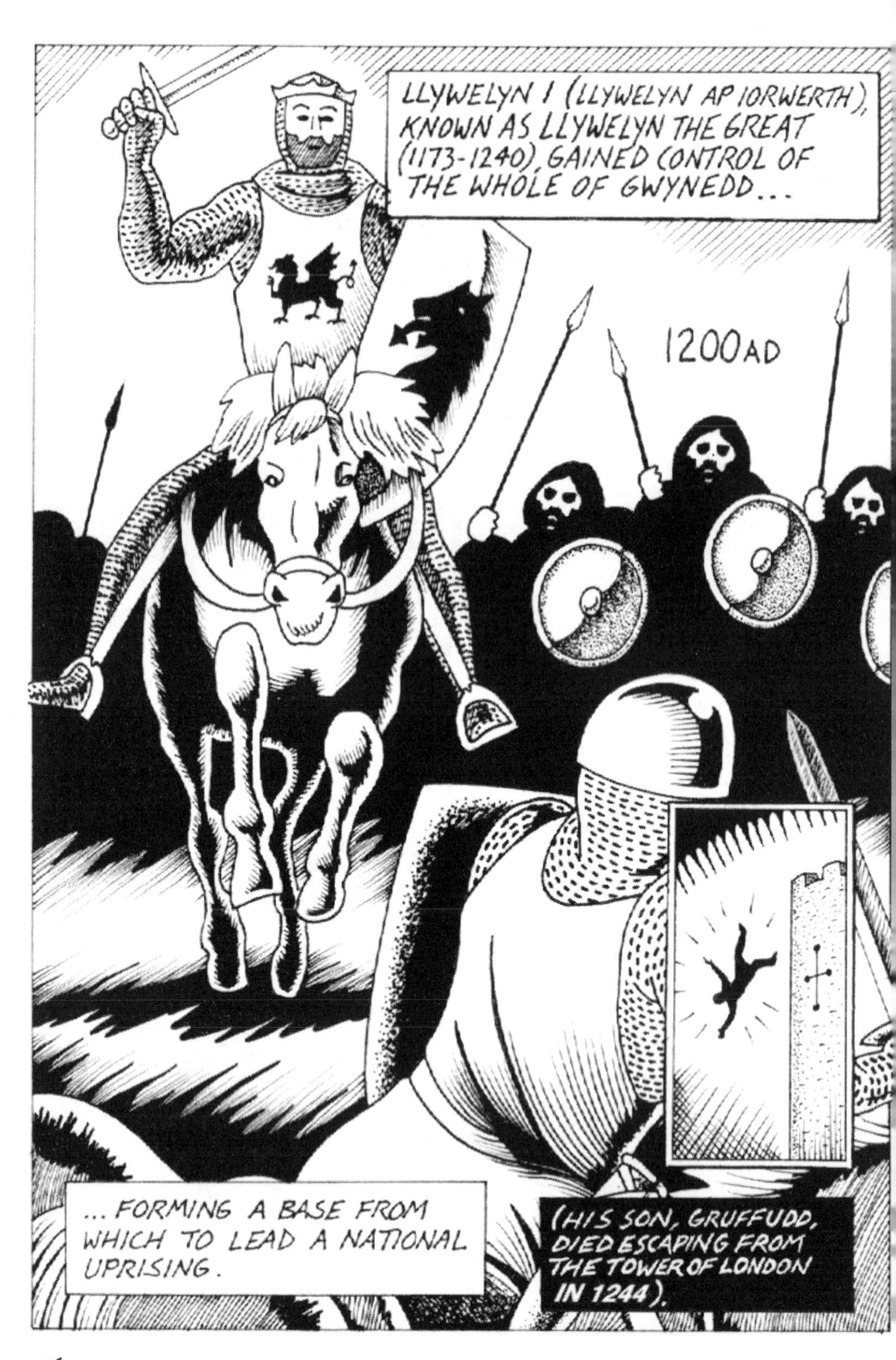
LLYWELYN I (LLYWELYN AP IORWERTH), KNOWN AS LLYWELYN THE GREAT (1173-1240), GAINED CONTROL OF THE WHOLE OF GWYNEDD...
1200AD
...FORMING A BASE FROM WHICH TO LEAD A NATIONAL UPRISING.
(HIS SON, GRUFFUDD, DIED ESCAPING FROM THE TOWER OF LONDON IN 1244).

LYWELYN THE GREAT'S FAMILY

SQUABBLED FOR A LONG TIME OVER WHO SHOULD BE RULER. HE CONTESTED AND ROSE AGAINST HIS UNCLE, CYNAN, OVERCOMING OPPOSITION FROM HIS COUSIN, MAREDUDD, AND SOON ESTABLISHING RULE OVER ALL OF GWYNEDD.

HE THEN BROUGHT POWYS AND DEHEUBARTH UNDER HIS INFLUENCE, ESTABLISHING POWER THROUGHOUT PURA WALIA.

PLEDGED TO THE DAUGHTER OF KING JOHN, HE HAD RIGHTS ENDORSED IN THE MAGNA CARTA IN 1215.

BY 1234 HE MADE PEACE WITH HENRY III's JUDICAR, HUBERT DE BURGH.

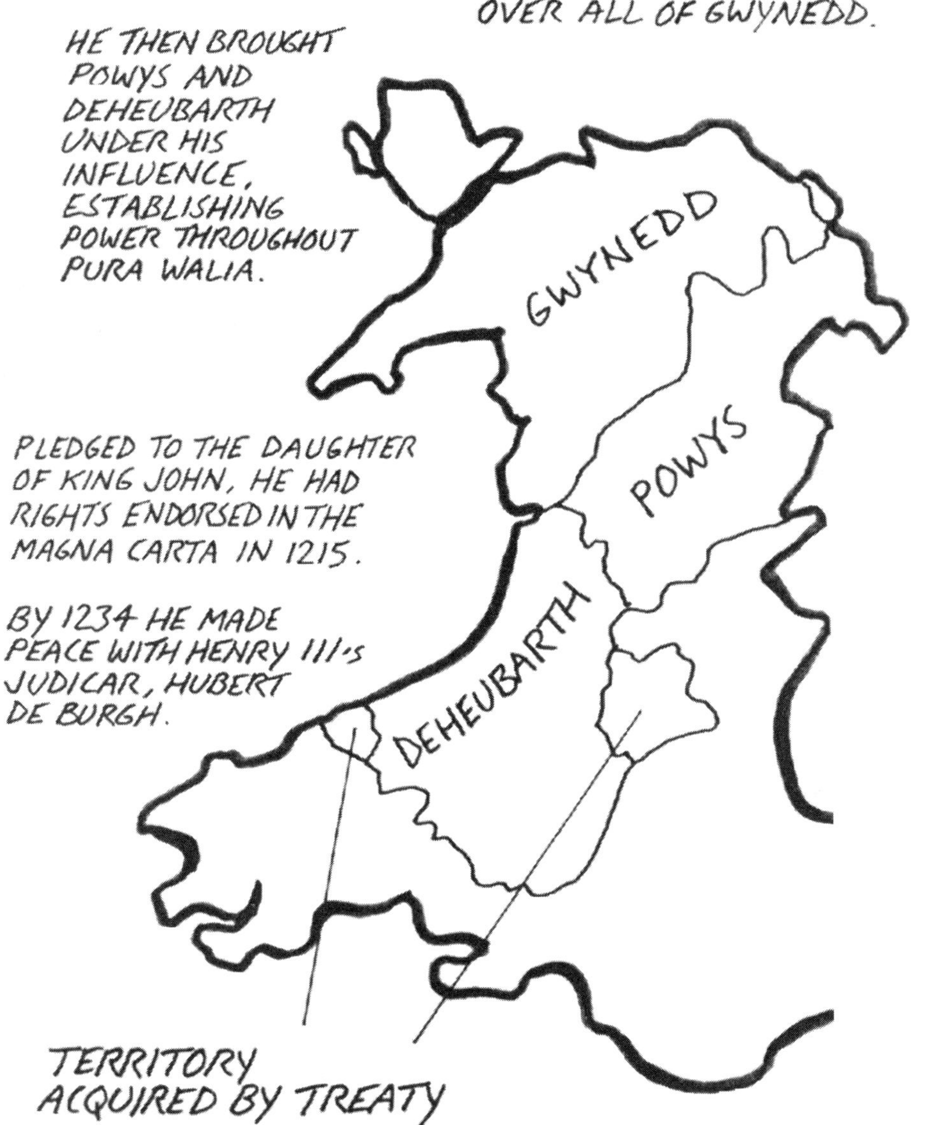

TERRITORY ACQUIRED BY TREATY

UNDER HIS GRANDSON, LLYWELYN II (LLYWELYN AP GRUFFUDD), KNOWN AS LLYWELYN THE LAST (1245-82), THE WELSH WENT ON TO REPOSSESS ALMOST ALL OF WALES.
AT THE HEIGHT OF HIS POWER, IN 1267, THE TREATY OF MONTGOMERY RECOGNISED WELSH INDEPENDENCE, AND ENGLAND'S HENRY III ACKNOWLEGED LLYWELYN II AS PRINCE OF WALES.

BUT ENGLAND'S EDWARD I QUICKLY AND BRUTALLY CONQUERED WALES IN 1282 ...
CRUSH THOSE WELSH ONCE AND FOR ALL!
... DETERMINED TO MAKE IT MORE SUB-SERVIENT TO ENGLAND THAN EVER BEFORE.
HE HAD ALREADY TRIED TO SUBDUE LLWYELYN 5 YEARS BEFORE.

LLYWELYN'S HEAD WAS SPIKED ON A LANCE OVER THE TOWER OF LONDON. HIS BROTHER DAVID CONTINUED THE REBELLION UNTIL HE TOO WAS CAPTURED...
...TO BE HUNG, DRAWN AND QUARTERED, HIS HEAD SPIKED AND PLACED BESIDE HIS BROTHER'S.

IN 1284, EDWARD CONFIRMED HIS HOLD ON WALES BY THE STATUTE OF RHUDDLAN, RESTRUCTURING THE ADMINISTRATION OF THE COUNTRY UNDER A TO-BE-APPOINTED PRINCE OF WALES...

WE WILL ONLY OBEY A PRINCE OF OUR OWN NATION, OF OUR OWN LANGUAGE AND WHOSE LIFE IS FREE FROM EVIL DEEDS.

GURGLE.

MEET YOUR NEW PRINCE: EDWARD. HE WAS BORN IN CAERNARFON, SPEAKS NOT A WORD OF ENGLISH AND HIS LIFE IS IMMACULATE!

FOR EDWARD, IT WAS NOT ENOUGH THAT WALES SHOULD BE A VASSAL STATE OF ENGLAND.
I WILL DESTROY WELSH NATIONHOOD FOR EVER!
IN 1301 HE PROCLAIMED HIS SON EDWARD 'PRINCE OF WALES'.
FROM THEN ONWARDS, THIS TITLE WOULD LIE WITH THE ELDEST SON OF THE ENGLISH MONARCH.

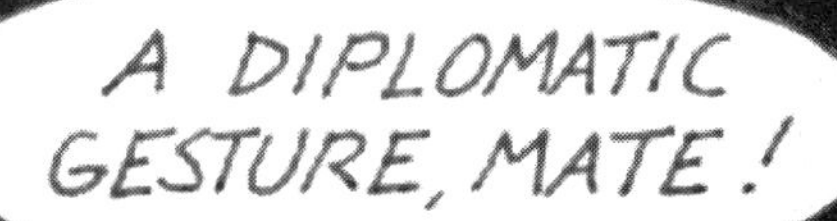

REBELLION CONTINUED, HOWEVER. THE UPRISINGS OF MADOG AP LLYWELYN (1294) AND LLYWELYN BREN (1311) GAVE EXPRESSION TO A SEETHING UNDERCURRENT OF NATIONAL OUTRAGE, ONLY TO MEET SUPPRESSION AND DEFEAT.

THEN, IN 1400, CAME THE MOST IMPORTANT AND OUTSTANDING NATIONAL UPRISING IN WELSH HISTORY (AND ONE OF THE MOST STRIKING IN THE MEDIAEVAL WORLD)...

chapter four

IN SEPTEMBER 1400, A FEUD WITH A NEIGHBOURING NOBLE, LORD GREY OF RUTHIN, STARTED OFF AN UPRISING.
THE INSURGENCY QUICKLY SPREAD THROUGHOUT THE WHOLE OF WALES. THE ENTIRE COUNTRY, WITH A SINGLE IDENTITY, UNITED IN THE STRUGGLE FOR NATIONAL INDEPENDENCE.
GLYNDŴR MEANWHILE FORMED POWERFUL ALLIANCES AGAINST ENGLAND'S HENRY IV WITH ENGLISH AND ANGLO-WELSH NOBLES WHO CHALLENGED HENRY'S DYNASTY...
NAMELY PERCY, EARL OF NORTHUMBERLAND; HIS HEIR, HENRY PERCY ('HOTSPUR'), AND EDMUND MORTIMER, AN ANGLO-WELSH NOBLE OF NORMAN DESCENT WHOSE NEPHEW HAD CLAIM TO THE ENGLISH THRONE.

BY THE END OF THE YEAR, MOST OF WALES WAS LIBERATED FROM ENGLISH RULE.
GLYNDŴR SET UP A PERIPATETIC WELSH PARLIAMENT, WITH REPRESENTATIVES FROM ALL PARTS OF WALES, MEETING AT HARLECH, DOLGELLAU, PENNAL AND MACHYNLLETH. PARLIAMENT ESTABLISHED A WELSH STATE, FORMULATING LAWS, NATIONAL INSTITUTIONS AND FOREIGN POLICY.

(THOUGH CONDITIONS OF WAR DID NOT ALLOW FOR A PERMANENT CENTRE WHERE PARLIAMENT COULD BE ESTABLISHED).
WE SHALL ESTABLISH TWO UNIVERSITIES – ONE FOR THE NORTH OF WALES AND ONE FOR THE SOUTH!

IN 1404, HIS ARMIES SEIZED THE GREAT ROYAL CASTLES OF HARLECH AND ABER-YSTWYTH.

CRUNCH
THUNK

FRENCH REINFORCEMENTS FAILED TO SAVE THE DAY, AND BY 1409 ALL THE MAIN WELSH STRONGHOLDS HAD BEEN RECAPTURED BY THE ENGLISH.

OWAIN GLYNDŴR CONTINUED TO LEAD GUERRILLA WARFARE UNTIL 1412, BUT THEN DISAPPEARED INTO HISTORY, HIS FATE AND WHEREABOUTS UNKNOWN TO THIS DAY.
I WILL RETURN!
THE UPRISING LEFT AN EVERLASTING FOLK MEMORY ON THE WELSH NATIONAL PSYCHE, AND A SPIRIT TO BE ECHOED IN LABOUR STRUGGLES CENTURIES LATER.

chapter five

DISLOYAL WELSHMEN WERE FORBIDDEN THE USE OF WEAPONS.
NO WELSH PERSON COULD HOLD AN OFFICIAL POST OR SERVE ON JURIES.
WE ARE THE **LAW**!
YES— ENGLISH LAW.

MARRIAGE BETWEEN ANY WELSH AND ENGLISH PERSONS WAS FORBIDDEN.
HOLD THE WEDDING!

WALES WAS DRAWN INTO ENGLAND'S 'WAR OF THE ROSES' (A CIVIL WAR OVER ROYAL SUCCESSION). THE OUTCOME WAS THE SUCCESSION OF A WELSHMAN TO THE THRONE OF ENGLAND – HENRY VII, FIRST OF THE TUDOR DYNASTY, BORN IN PEMBROKE CASTLE.
PEMBROKE DOCK HARLEQUINS R.F.C.
A WELSHMAN IN POWER? MAYBE HE'LL LOOK AFTER OUR INTERESTS.
HMMM. WE'LL SEE.

THE WELSH LANGUAGE WAS PROSCRIBED FOR OFFICIAL PURPOSES. ENGLISH LAW AND RELIGION WERE IMPOSED, WALES BEING DENIED AN INDEPENDENT CHURCH, LEGAL AND EDUCATION SYSTEM. WELSH STUDENTS HAD TO GO TO ENGLISH UNIVERSITIES RIGHT UP UNTIL THE LATE 19th CENTURY.

ANGLESEY
FLINTSHIRE
DENBIGHSHIRE
CAERNARVONSHIRE
MERIONETHSHIRE
FLINTSHIRE
MONTGOMERY-
SHIRE
CARDIGANSHIRE
RADNORSHIRE
BRECKNOCKSHIRE
PEMBROKE-
SHIRE
CARMARTHENSHIRE
GLAMORGANSHIRE
MONMOUTH-
SHIRE
ACT OF UNION,
1536
THIS ACT (AND SUBSEQUENT ACTS) ABSORBED WALES INTO THE ADMINISTRATIVE AND LEGAL SYSTEMS OF ENGLAND. THE ABOVE COUNTIES WERE FORMED, REMAINING UNTIL 1974.

IN 1642 BEGAN THE ENGLISH CIVIL WAR BETWEEN THE PARLIAMENTARIANS ('ROUNDHEADS'), LED BY OLIVER CROMWELL...
VICTORY TO THE COMMONWEALTH AND AN ELECTED PARLIAMENT!
VICTORY TO THE KING!
...AND THE ROYALISTS ('CAVALIERS'), LED BY CHARLES I.

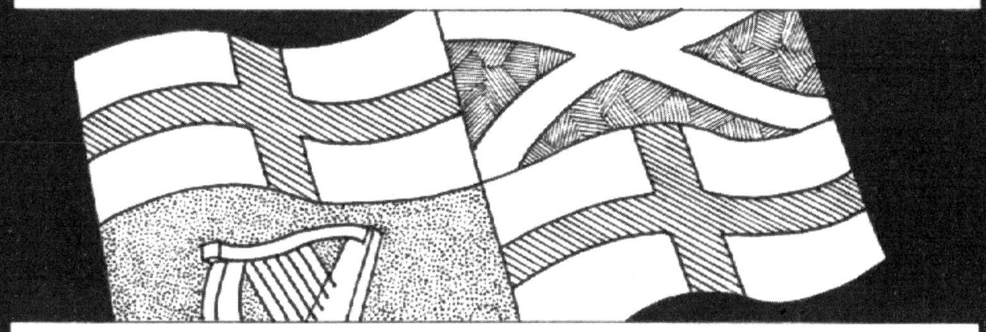
MOST OF THE ARISTOCRACY IN WALES SUPPORTED THE KING, AND WALES WAS DRAWN INTO THE WAR. THE PARLIAMENTARIANS WON AND WALES BECAME PART OF THE COMMONWEALTH, BUT WAS UNDER-REPRESENTED IN PARLIAMENT. THE WELSH FLAG, JUST LIKE TODAY, WAS NOT REPRESENTED ON THE BRITISH FLAG.

CROMWELL'S RULE WAS STRICT. HE DISSOLVED THE PARLIAMENT, BECOMING 'LORD PROTECTOR'— A MILITARY DICTATOR.

THE RESTORATION IN 1660 BROUGHT BACK THE MONARCHY. SCOTLAND, WHICH HAD BEEN PART OF THE COMMONWEALTH, REGAINED ITS INDEPENDENCE. WALES DID NOT.

chapter six

ALL THIS MADE LITTLE DIFFERENCE TO THE AVERAGE WELSH PEASANT, LIVING IN POVERTY AND SPEAKING WELSH. THE UPPER CLASS WAS ENGLISH OR ANGLICISED AND THE LITERATE MIDDLE CLASS READ BOOKS PRINTED IN ENGLAND. THEN, IN THE 18th CENTURY, BEGAN A PHENOMENON WHICH WOULD GREATLY INFLUENCE WELSH SOCIETY FOR A LONG TIME TO COME: **RELIGIOUS REVIVALISM**.

IT IS APPARENT THAT, WHILE THE STIRRINGS OF SOCIAL REVOLUTION WERE AFFECTING MUCH OF EUROPE, NONCONFORMIST ANTI-CLERICALISM TRANSFERRED POTENTIAL REVOLUTION IN WALES INTO A MASS RELIGIOUS MOVEMENT. ORIGINALLY A PROTEST MOVEMENT AGAINST THE ANGLICAN ESTABLISHMENT, NONCONFORMITY WOULD INDEED BECOME A WELSH ESTABLISHMENT IN ITS OWN RIGHT.

THE STEREOTYPED WELSH IMAGE OF CHAPELS AND SUNDAY TEETOTALISM IS A CLICHÉ THAT PERSISTED ALMOST TO THE END OF THE 20th CENTURY, EVEN AFTER IT WAS NO LONGER ACCURATE.

NEVERTHELESS, NONCONFORMITY SPREAD LITERACY AMONG THE COMMON PEOPLE AND HELPED OPEN THE WAY FOR DEMOCRATIC AND DECENTRALIST IDEAS AND TRADITIONS. ITS CLERGY OR LEADERS WERE DRAWN FROM THE LOWER CLASSES. **IT HELPED GIVE THE WELSH WORKING PEOPLE AN IDENTITY WHILE THEIR RULING CLASS EMBRACED THE CHURCH OF ENGLAND**. THOUGH HARDLY A REVOLUTIONARY MOVEMENT, IT TAUGHT PEOPLE HOW TO ORGANISE THEMSELVES AND TO MAKE SPEECHES. MANY LEADING LIBERALS AND POLITICAL ORATORS WERE NONCONFORMISTS AND THE MOVEMENT INFLUENCED THE LIBERALISM WHICH WOULD DOMINATE WELSH POLITICS FOR MANY YEARS.

MEANWHILE, POPULAR DISCONTENT— FOOD RIOTS— OCCURRED THROUGH-OUT THE 18th CENTURY...
...AS PEASANTS, COTTAGERS AND WORKERS, FACED WITH STARVATION, REBELLED AGAINST HIGH PRICES, RENTS AND TAXES.
IN DUE COURSE, SUCH DESPERATE ACTION WOULD BECOME MORE ORGANISED, DEMANDING DEMOCRATIC GOVERNMENT AND AN END TO POVERTY AND INEQUALITY. EARLY TRADES UNIONS ('COMBINATIONS') WERE FORMED, AND WERE SUPPRESSED BY LAW.

BY THE LATTER PART OF THE CENTURY, THE POLITICAL WIND OF RADICALISM IN EUROPE AND THE AMERICAN COLONIES HAD REACHED WALES.
THE WELSH ENLIGHTENMENT HAD BEGUN.
MANY WELSH INTELLECTUALS SUPPORTED AND PARTICIPATED IN THE AMERICAN AND FRENCH REVOLUTIONS, FIGHTING FOR REPUBLICAN, DEMOCRATIC IDEALS.
MANY SIGNATORIES OF THE AMERICAN DECLARATION OF INDEPENDENCE WERE OF WELSH ORIGIN OR BACKGROUND.

WITHOUT ITS OWN CULTURE, WALES WILL LOSE ITS IDENTITY.
WE MUST KEEP OUR SOUL!
NATIONAL POET IOLO MORGANWG (EDWARD WILLIAMS) INFLUENCED HIS CONTEMPORARIES BY EXPRESSING LIBERTARIAN RADICAL IDEALS IN HIS WORKS, TOGETHER WITH A STRONG NATIONAL AWARENESS.
HE WAS ONE OF THE LEADING FIGURES IN A REVIVAL OF NATIONAL CULTURE AT THE TIME, NOW KNOWN AS THE WELSH RENAISSANCE.

IOLO MORGANWG INSTIGATED THE NATIONAL EISTEDDFOD, WALES' ANNUAL CULTURAL FESTIVAL.

MORGANWG (1747-1826) WAS A CLOSE ASSOCIATE OF THE 'GWYNEDDIGION', A WELSH PATRIOT SOCIETY IN LONDON, FOUNDED IN 1770.

DR. RICHARD PRICE, THE GREAT WELSH POLITICAL THEORIST, WAS A CLOSE FRIEND OF BENJAMIN FRANKLIN IN LONDON.

HIS ADVANCED, DEMOCRATIC VIEWS INFLUENCED THE FRENCH REVOLUTIONARIES.

DR. PRICE DIED IN 1791.

ANOTHER WELSH REVOLUTIONARY, DAVID WILLIAMS, PUBLISHED IN 1782 HIS 'LETTERS ON POLITICAL LIBERTY', SO DYNAMIC THAT ITS FRENCH TRANSLATOR WAS SENT TO THE BASTILLE BY THE ROYALISTS.
LIBERTÉ EGALITÉ FRATERNITÉ
ET SORORITÉ!
AFTER THE REVOLUTION, WILLIAMS HELPED ORGANISE THE CONSTITUTION OF THE NEW FRANCE. HE WAS MADE AN HONORARY CITIZEN OF THE FRENCH REPUBLIC AND WAS ADMIRED BY LEADING ACTIVISTS SUCH AS VOLTAIRE AND ROUSSEAU.

BUT IN FEBRUARY 1787, REPUBLICAN FRANCE DECIDED TO ATTACK ENGLAND. CONSIDERING WELSH SYMPATHISERS, THEY ERRONEOUSLY THOUGHT WALES WOULD BE A GOOD PLACE TO LAND AN EXPEDITIONARY FORCE, EXPECTING WELSH SUPPORT AGAINST ENGLAND.
J'ARRIVE!
THEY LANDED IN FISHGUARD BAY, LOOTING AND DRINKING, BUT WERE RESISTED BY THE LOCAL POPULATION.
WHEN REGULAR TROOPS ARRIVED, THE FRENCH FORCE WAS DEFEATED, WITH FEW CASUALTIES. THE INVASION, TOGETHER WITH THE BLOODSHED IN FRANCE AND THE RISE OF NAPOLEON, IMPAIRED WELSH SYMPATHY FOR FRANCE, THOUGH THE ENGLISH ESTABLISHMENT CONTINUED TO REGARD THE WELSH WITH SUSPICION.

DURING BRITAIN'S WARS WITH REPUBLICAN AND NAPOLEONIC FRANCE, ALL RADICALISM WAS RUTHLESSLY SUPPRESSED. CENSORSHIP FORBADE ALL 'SEDITIOUS' WRITINGS AND MEETINGS.
RHYDDID
FACED WITH SUCH FRUSTRATION, MORGAN JOHN RHYS (A PREACHER WHO HAD PUBLISHED A PIONEERING RADICAL 'WELSH JOURNAL') TOOK HIS FOLLOWERS TO AMERICA IN 1794, ATTEMPTING TO SET UP A DEMOCRATIC WELSH HOMELAND THERE.
HIS MISSION FAILED, HOWEVER, HIS 'BEULAH' COMMUNITY ILL-PLANNED AND UNSUCCESSFUL.

JAC GLAN Y GORS (1766-1821), A WELSH EXPATRIATE LIVING IN LONDON, RAN A TAVERN IN SOUTHWARK WHERE LONDON'S WELSH RADICAL CIRCLES MET REGULARLY.
DOWN WITH MONARCHY AND ARISTOCRACY! DOWN WITH THE GENTRY!
HERE'S TO UNIVERSAL DEMOCRACY AND AN END TO CLASS PRIVILEGE!

THE WELSH JACOBINS
CIVIL LIBERTY AND EQUAL RIGHTS FOR ALL!
HERE'S TO THE WELSH REPUBLIC!
AFTER THE PUBLICATION OF TWO WELSH REVOLUTIONARY PAMPHLETS, 'SEREN TAN GWMWL' (THE STAR BEHIND A CLOUD) AND 'TORIAD Y DYDD' (DAYBREAK), CONTROVERSY AROSE AND JAC WAS FORCED TO FLEE LONDON.

chapter seven

IN THE COUNTRY, 'ENCLOSURE' OF LAND MEANT PREVIOUSLY COMMON LAND BECOMING THE PRIVATE PROPERTY OF BIG LANDOWNERS AND LARGE, SUCCESSFUL FARMERS.
OUTBREAKS OF RURAL VIOLENCE AGAINST THE CHANGES OCCURRED THROUGHOUT MUCH OF WALES, NOTABLY AT MYNYDD BACH, CARDIGANSHIRE, WHERE 600 PEASANTS DESTROYED THE HOUSES AND FENCES OF AN ENGLISH LANDOWNER IN WHAT BECAME KNOWN AS 'RHYFEL Y SAIS BACH'– THE WAR OF THE LITTLE ENGLISHMAN.

LANDOWNERS' AND INDUSTRIALISTS' MANSIONS OVERLOOKED THE GRIMY INDUSTRIAL TOWNS IN THE VALLEYS, WHERE THE POOR AND DISPOSSESSED FLOCKED TO WORK IN THE IRONWORKS, MINES, FACTORIES AND DOCKS, FORMING THE WELSH WORKING CLASS.

CHILDREN, WOMEN AND MEN WORKED IN APPALLING CONDITIONS. ANGER OFTEN EXPLODED INTO STRIKES, RIOTS AND ACTS OF SABOTAGE...

BUT THE ORGANISATION OF TRADES UNIONS TO PROTECT AND PROMOTE WORKERS' RIGHTS WAS HINDERED BY THE PHYSICAL GEOGRAPHY OF THE LAND.

HOWEVER, WORKERS IN MONMOUTHSHIRE IN THE 1820's FORMED ANOTHER TYPE OF ORGANISATION TO ENSURE JUSTICE...

FROM THEIR BEGINNINGS IN THE 1820'S, THE **'SCOTCH CATTLE'** REACHED THEIR ZENITH IN THE EARLY 1830'S, CONTINUING THEIR ACTIVITIES UNTIL THE MIDDLE OF THE DECADE.

ENEMIES OF THE CATTLE WERE THREATENED WITH STERN WARNING LETTERS. IF THESE WERE IGNORED...
WHAT'S THIS? 'O LORD LOOK ON THY SITUATION, YOU DAMNED TOAD, FOR YOU SHALL BE IN HELL BEFORE MONDAY MORNING...
... AND YOUR HEART FIXED ON THE HORNS OF THE BULL'. OH YES, TERRIFYING I'M SURE.
OPEN UP!
MOOOOOOOO
BANG!
THUMP!
MOOOOOO

UFFERN DÂN!

...THEY WOULD BE VISITED IN THE NIGHT BY 'HERDS' OF HEAVILY DISGUISED MEN.
CRASH
WE'VE COME FOR YOU, SGUM!
THE HERD WOULD ANNOUNCE THEIR APPROACH WITH HORNS, GUNS AND LOWING NOISES, AND THEIR LEADER, THE 'TARW' OR BULL, WORE A HORNED MASK.

THE CATTLE WOULD THEN 'DUFF UP' THEIR VICTIMS, SMASH WINDOWS AND FURNITURE, THEN LEAVE AS MYSTERIOUSLY AS THEY HAD COME.
WE HATE THE PROFITEERING BOSSES!
BUT WE HATE CLASS TRAITORS EVEN MORE!
ONE THING YOU DO NOT DO IS BETRAY YOUR OWN KIND!
ER... DO YOU REALISE THIS IS ILLEGAL?
ONE CATTLE ACTIVIST, A MINER CALLED EDWARD MORGAN, WAS CAUGHT AND HANGED AT MONMOUTH GAOL IN 1835, WHEREAFTER ACTIVITY RECEDED, BUT OCCASIONAL SCOTCH CATTLE ATTACKS CONTINUED UNTIL 1850.

chapter eight

MEANWHILE, A MORE SIGNIFICANT EVENT HAD TAKEN PLACE:
THE MERTHYR RISING (1831).

WAUN HILL, MERTHYR, MAY 30TH 1831...
5000 PEOPLE DEMONSTRATED.
LET US CLAIM OUR DEMOCRATIC RIGHTS!
THE CAMPAIGN CONTINUED FOR TWO DAYS, WHEN THE CROWD MOVED ON TO MORE DIRECT ACTION...

REFORM FOR EVER!
DESTROY THE DEBTORS' COURT!
THIS ISN'T LOOTING.
WE'RE ONLY TAKING BACK WHAT ALREADY BELONGS TO US.
SEQUESTRATED GOODS WERE RETURNED TO THEIR OWNERS.

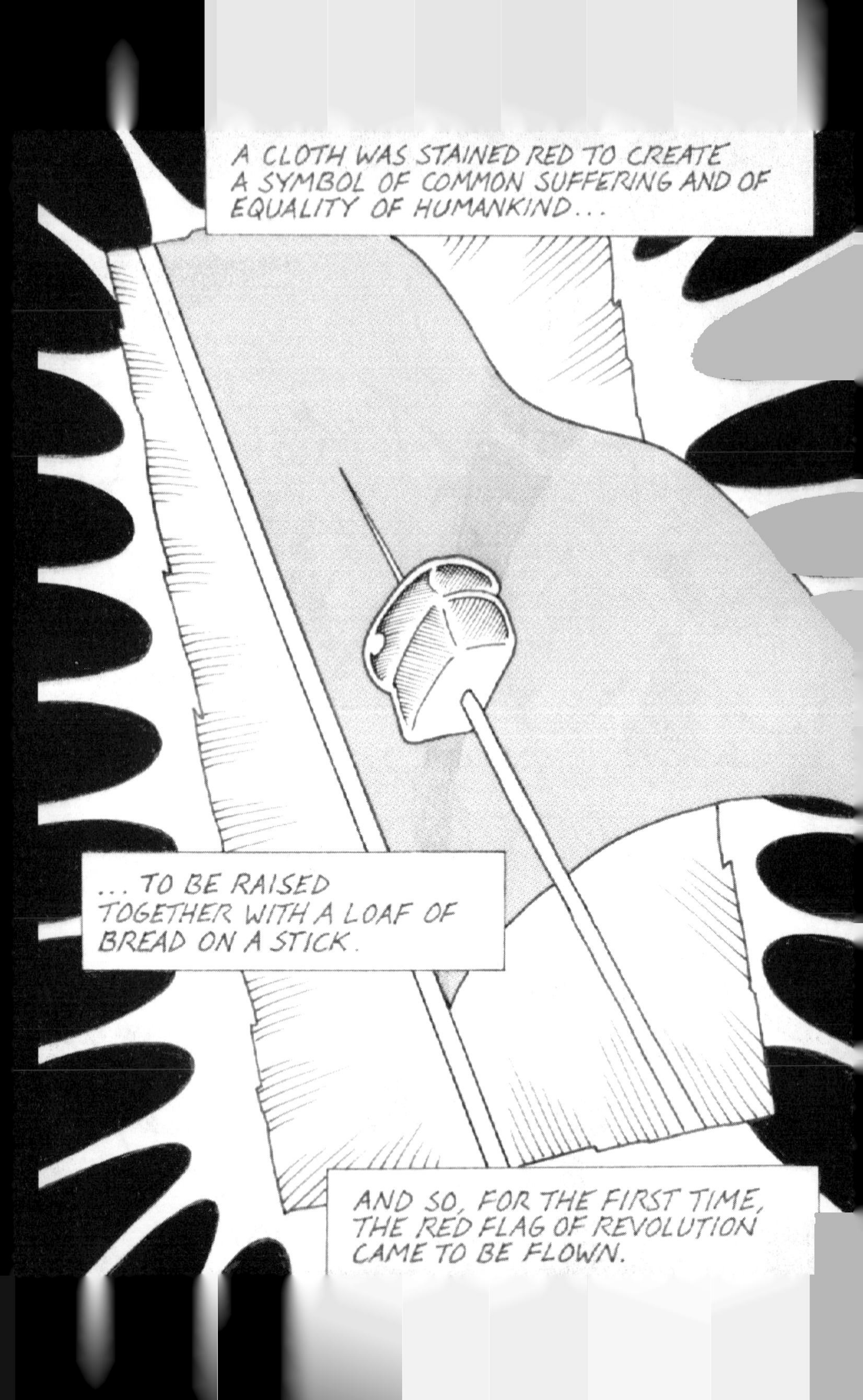
A CLOTH WAS STAINED RED TO CREATE A SYMBOL OF COMMON SUFFERING AND OF EQUALITY OF HUMANKIND...
... TO BE RAISED TOGETHER WITH A LOAF OF BREAD ON A STICK.
AND SO, FOR THE FIRST TIME, THE RED FLAG OF REVOLUTION CAME TO BE FLOWN.

LOCAL JUSTICES SENT FOR TROOPS FROM BRECON GARRISON.
SOLDIERS FROM A SCOTTISH HIGHLAND REGIMENT WERE STATIONED AT THE CASTLE INN.
THE MILITARY OCCUPIED MERTHYR AND THERE FOLLOWED A GENERAL STRIKE.

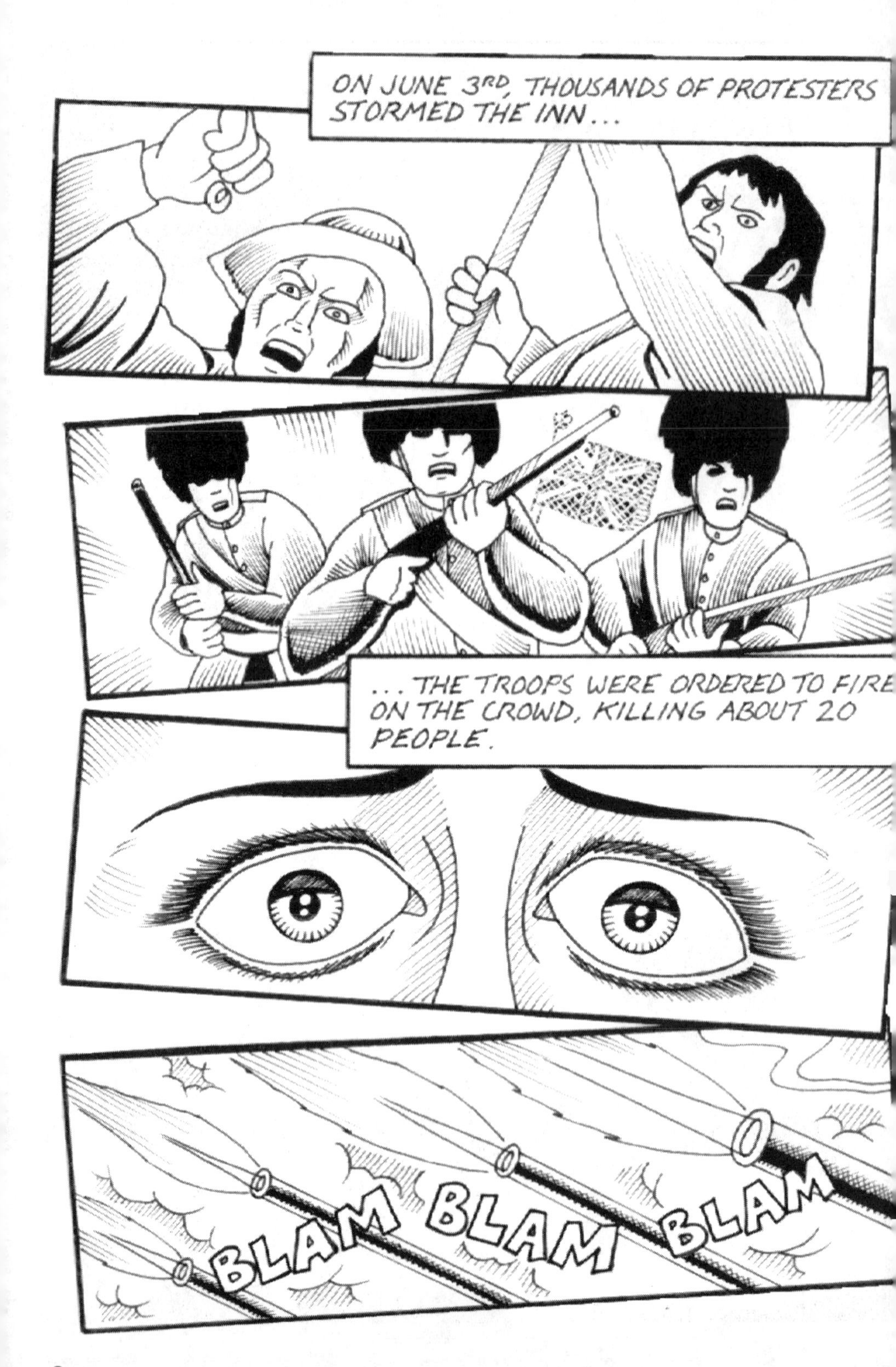
ON JUNE 3RD, THOUSANDS OF PROTESTERS STORMED THE INN...
...THE TROOPS WERE ORDERED TO FIRE ON THE CROWD, KILLING ABOUT 20 PEOPLE.
BLAM BLAM BLAM

BUT THE RIOTERS BECAME ORGANISED, SETTING UP CAMP AT CEFNCOED Y CYMER AND DRILLING UNDER THE RED FLAG.
THE PEOPLE ARE RISING. SUPPORT IS WIDESPREAD.

LET'S PREPARE TO MARCH ON SWANSEA AND CARDIFF!

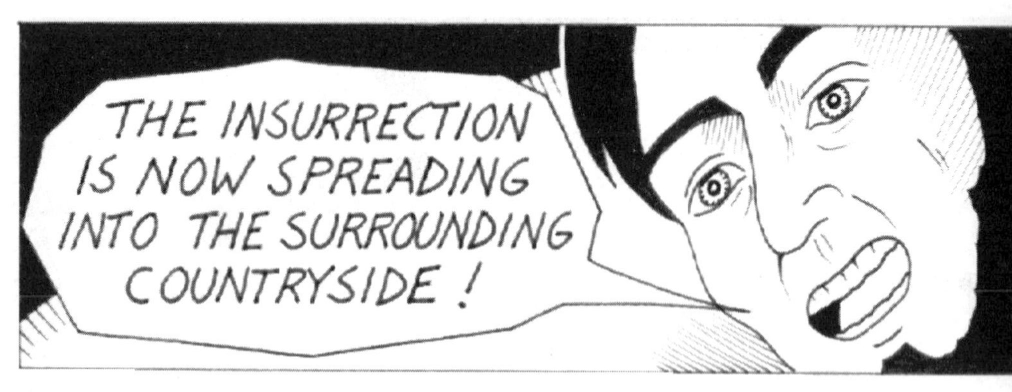
THE INSURRECTION IS NOW SPREADING INTO THE SURROUNDING COUNTRYSIDE !

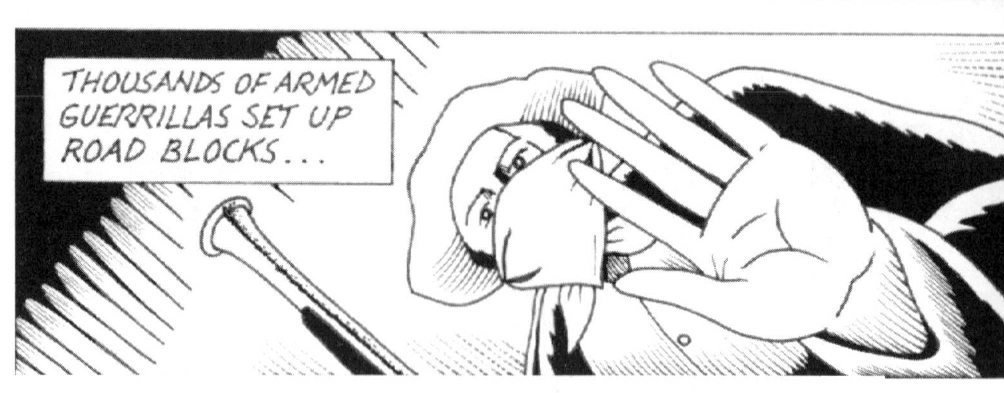
THOUSANDS OF ARMED GUERRILLAS SET UP ROAD BLOCKS...

...AND DESTROYED HATED TRUCK SHOPS.
SMASH!

AS THE IRONMASTERS AND MINEOWNERS HID IN THEIR CASTLES AND PALACES, WORKERS TOOK REVENGE ON AGENTS AND MANAGERS.

THE NEXT DAY, MORE TROOPS WERE SENT FOR. A BODY OF SWANSEA CAVALRY WAS STOPPED BY RIOTERS AND FORCED TO SURRENDER THEIR WEAPONS BEFORE BEING ALLOWED TO DEPART, UNHARMED.
HAND OVER YOUR WEAPONS!
ALL RIGHT. NOW GET OUT OF HERE.
CLATTER

ONLY AFTER MORE REGULAR TROOPS ARRIVED, AND TWO PITCHED BATTLES FOUGHT, WAS ORDER REIMPOSED. BY SATURDAY 7th, THE RISING WAS CRUSHED.

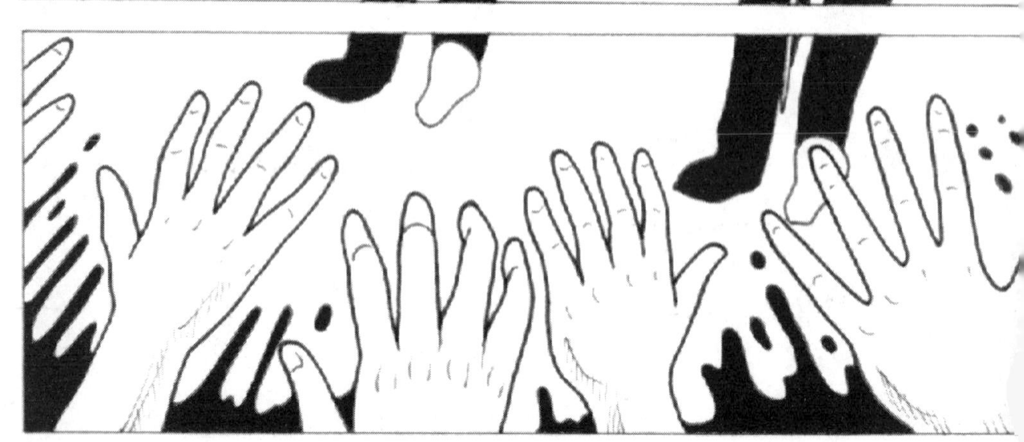

EVENTUALLY, 18 RINGLEADERS WERE ROUNDED UP, MOST OF THEM TO BE TRANSPORTED TO AUSTRALIA. TWO WERE SENTENCED TO DEATH: LEWIS LEWIS (KNOWN AS LEWSYN YR HELIWR - 'LEWIS THE HUNTSMAN'), WHO WAS LATER REPRIEVED AND SENTENCED TO TRANSPORTATION...
...AND RICHARD LEWIS, BETTER KNOWN AS DIC PENDERYN, A YOUNG MINER FROM ABERAFAN.

YOU ARE ACCUSED OF WOUNDING A SOLDIER OF THE CROWN. HOW DO YOU PLEAD?
NOT GUILTY!
DIC PROTESTED HIS INNOCENCE TO THE END...

... BUT WAS HANGED AT CARDIFF IN AUGUST 1831...

RICHARD LEWIS
'DIC PENDERYN'
...AND TO THIS DAY REMAINS AN OUTSTANDING WELSH FOLK HERO AND WORKING-CLASS MARTYR.

chapter nine

A REFORM ACT OF 1831 EXTENDED VOTING RIGHTS FOR THE INDUSTRIAL BOURGEOISIE AND AFFLUENT MIDDLE CLASSES, WHO COULD NOW POWER-SHARE WITH THE LANDED GENTRY. THE WELSH MAJORITY STILL HAD NO VOTE.

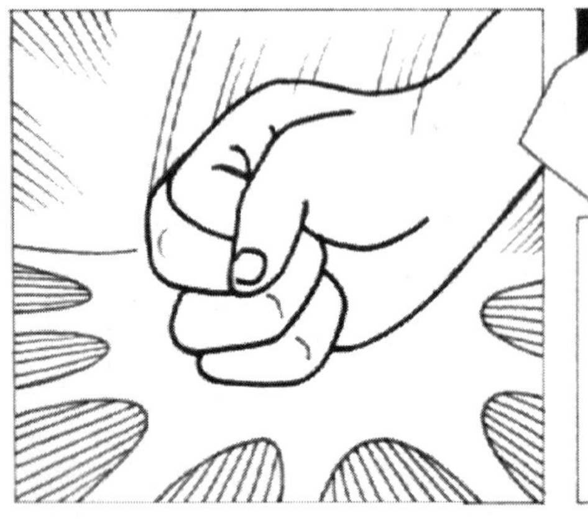

CHARTISM, DEMANDING WORKERS' VOTING RIGHTS AND ANNUAL GENERAL ELECTIONS, NATURALLY APPEALED TO THE WELSH, BUT WELSH CHARTISTS WERE ESPECIALLY MILITANT.

AT LLANIDLOES IN 1839, CHARTIST WEAVERS HELD VIOLENT DEMONSTRATIONS. EXTRA POLICE WERE BROUGHT IN, STATIONED AT THE TREWYTHEN ARMS.
THE WORKERS ATTACKED THE INN, OVERPOWERING THE POLICE. THE CHARTISTS CONTROLLED THE TOWN FOR A WEEK.
DON'T SHOOT!
WE SURRENDER
BUT TROOPS ARRIVED FROM BRECON AND SUPPRESSED THE REVOLT.

THE LEADERS WERE TRANSPORTED AND LONDON CHARTIST ORGANISER HENRY VINCENT JAILED IN MONMOUTH.
MONMOUTHSHIRE CHARTISTS NOW TOOK ACTION.
WEAPONS AND AMMUNITION WERE STORED IN CAVES AND MEETINGS HELD IN PUBS.

ON OCTOBER 3rd, AT A SECRET MEETING IN THE VILLAGE OF BLACKWOOD, RHYMNEY VALLEY, AN INVASION OF NEWPORT WAS PLANNED.

RIGHT! WE'LL MEET UP AT CEFN ON THE 4th OF NOVEMBER AND GO ON TO TAKE NEWPORT!

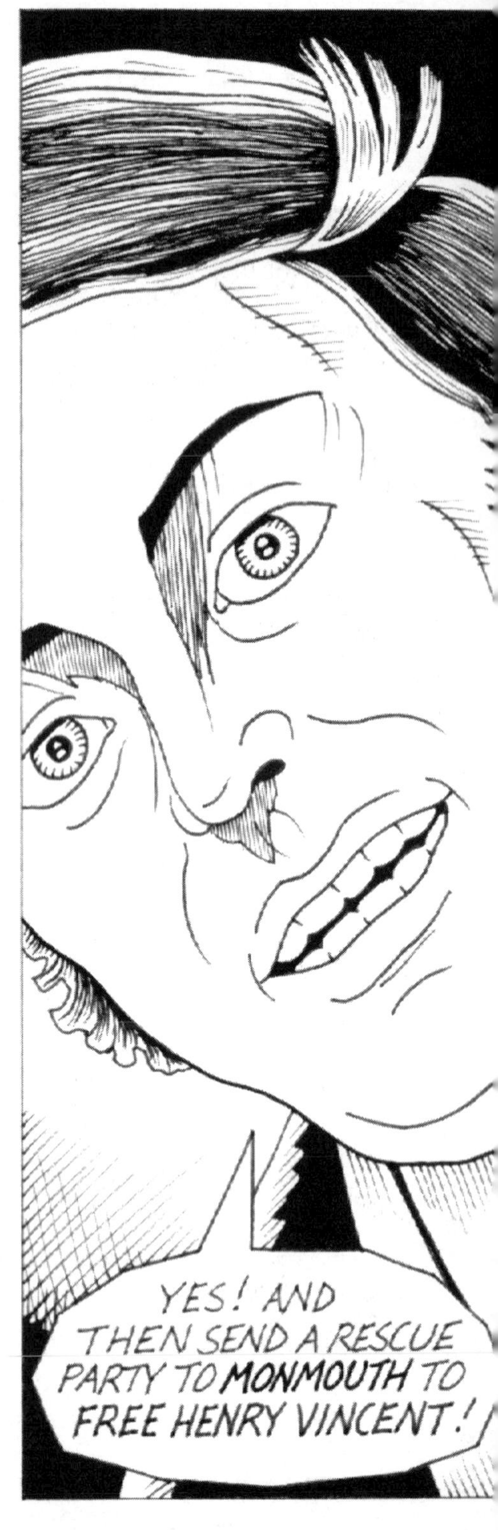
YES! AND THEN SEND A RESCUE PARTY TO MONMOUTH TO FREE HENRY VINCENT!

ON THE ACTUAL NIGHT, THE PONTYPOOL CONTINGENT, THROUGH POOR ORGANISATION, FAILED TO TURN UP. THE REMAINING COLUMNS ADVANCED AS PLANNED, DESPITE BAD WEATHER.
BY THE TIME THEY REACHED NEWPORT, THE AUTHORITIES HAD BEEN ALERTED. TROOPS WERE STATIONED AT THE WESTGATE HOTEL.

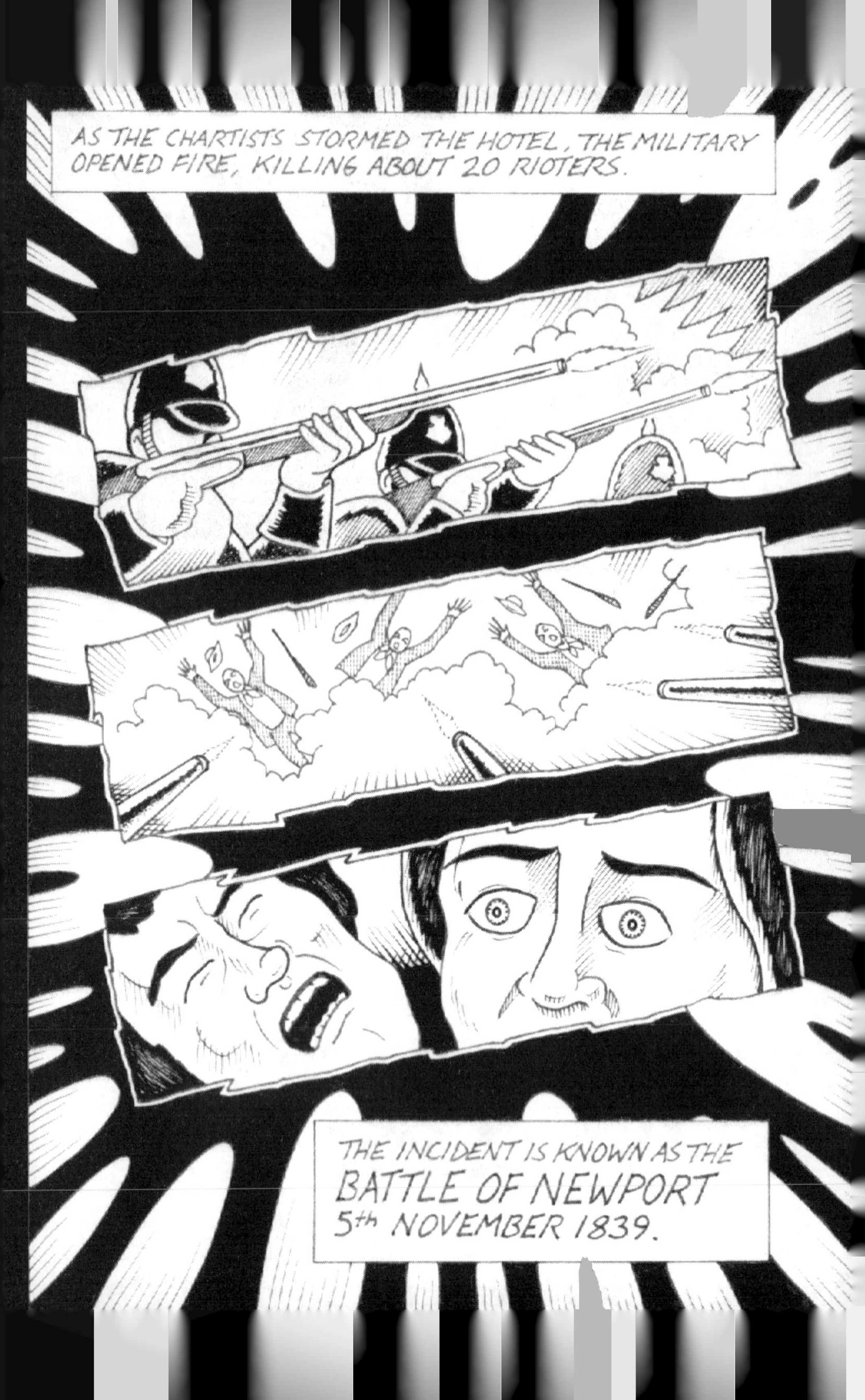
AS THE CHARTISTS STORMED THE HOTEL, THE MILITARY OPENED FIRE, KILLING ABOUT 20 RIOTERS.
THE INCIDENT IS KNOWN AS THE BATTLE OF NEWPORT 5th NOVEMBER 1839.

AFTERWARDS, 8 MEN WERE CHARGED WITH HIGH TREASON.
YOU ARE SENTENCED TO BE HUNG, DRAWN AND QUARTERED!
BUT THEIR SENTENCES WERE COMMUTED...
VERY WELL, THEN. TRANSPORTATION FOR LIFE! (WE'RE TOO DAMNED LIBERAL).
THE REMISSION OF THE DEATH PENALTY MAY HAVE ABATED FURTHER ARMED REBELLION, BUT THE PUBLIC STILL CAMPAIGNED FOR THEIR HEROES' PARDON, 1,400 PEOPLE SIGNING PETITIONS FOR THEIR RELEASE.

EVENTUALLY, ALL WERE PARDONED (MOST DIED IN AUSTRALIA ANYWAY), BUT ONLY JOHN FROST, AT 70, RETURNED — TO A HERO'S WELCOME!

THE DISTURBANCE AT NEWPORT DID NOT GIVE WAY TO AN EXPECTED WELSH UPRISING, BUT PROTEST CONTINUED, IN THE COUNTRY AS WELL AS THE TOWNS. A NEW WAVE OF RIOTS HAD ALREADY BEGUN IN PEMBROKESHIRE AND CARMARTHENSHIRE, INITIALLY AGAINST EXTORTIONATE ROAD TOLLS...

The Rebecca Riots

chapter ten

'AND THEY BLESSED REBECCA, AND SAID UNTO HER, "THOU ART OUR SISTER ; BE THOU THE MOTHER OF THOUSANDS OF MILLIONS, AND LET THY DESCENDANTS POSSESS THE GATES OF THOSE WHO HATE THEM".'

GENESIS ch. 24 v. 60.

DUW!
WE RESENT PAYING HEAVY TOLLS FOR BAD ROADS!

SMASH THE ACCURSED TOLL GATE!

SMASH!
CHOP!

THE TOLL KEEPER AND HIS FAMILY WERE CHASED OUT AND THE TOLL HOUSE BURNED.
HOW COULD THEY?
BADLY BROUGHT UP, I SUPPOSE
A NEW PHENOMENON HAD ARRIVED IN WELSH HISTORY: THE REBECCA RIOTS.

DISGUISED IN ROUGH WOMEN'S DRESSES (WORN OVER THEIR OWN WORKING-MEN'S CLOTHES), THEIR FACES BLACKENED WITH SOOT, THE REBECCA RIOTERS RODE THE COUNTRYSIDE BY NIGHT, DESTROYING ALL TOLL GATES.

LAUGH!
I DARE YOU!

THE 'DAUGHTERS OF REBECCA' HAD THE ENORMOUS SUPPORT OF THE WORKING POPULATION. BY 1843 THEY BEGAN TO MOVE INTO THE AREA OF POLITICAL PROTEST, DEMANDING DEMOCRATIC RIGHTS.

CARMARTHEN, 19 JUNE 1843
LET US MARCH TO THE GUILDHALL TO SEE THE MAYOR AND COUNCIL! LET US DEMAND JUSTICE!
FREEDOM
CYFIAWNDER
RHYDDID
BARA A CHAWS
MAGISTRATES PERSUADED THE DEMONSTRATORS TO LEAVE THEIR SHOTGUNS BEHIND, AND THE DEMONSTRATION WENT AHEAD. BUT THEN...

STORM THE WORKHOUSE!
SYMBOL OF OUR OPPRESSION AND DESPAIR!

"FREEDOM AND BETTER FOOD, FREE TOLLS AND LIBERTY".
RHYDDID A GWELL LLUNIAETH, TOLL RYDD A RHYDDID
DESTROY THE HATED WORKHOUSE!

ATTACK THE WORKHOUSE!
ANGER AMONG THE DESPERATE CARMARTHEN TOWNSFOLK BOILED OVER. THE DEMONSTRATION TURNED INTO A RIOT.
THE AUTHORITIES ACTED IMMEDIATELY
SEND FOR THE TROOPS!

THE 4th LIGHT DRAGOONS LAUNCHED THEIR FIRST CHARGE IN HISTORY (THEIR NEXT WOULD BE AT THE BATTLE OF BALACLAVA).
THE DRAGOONS QUELLED THE RIOT, BUT REBELLION CONTINUED TO SPREAD.

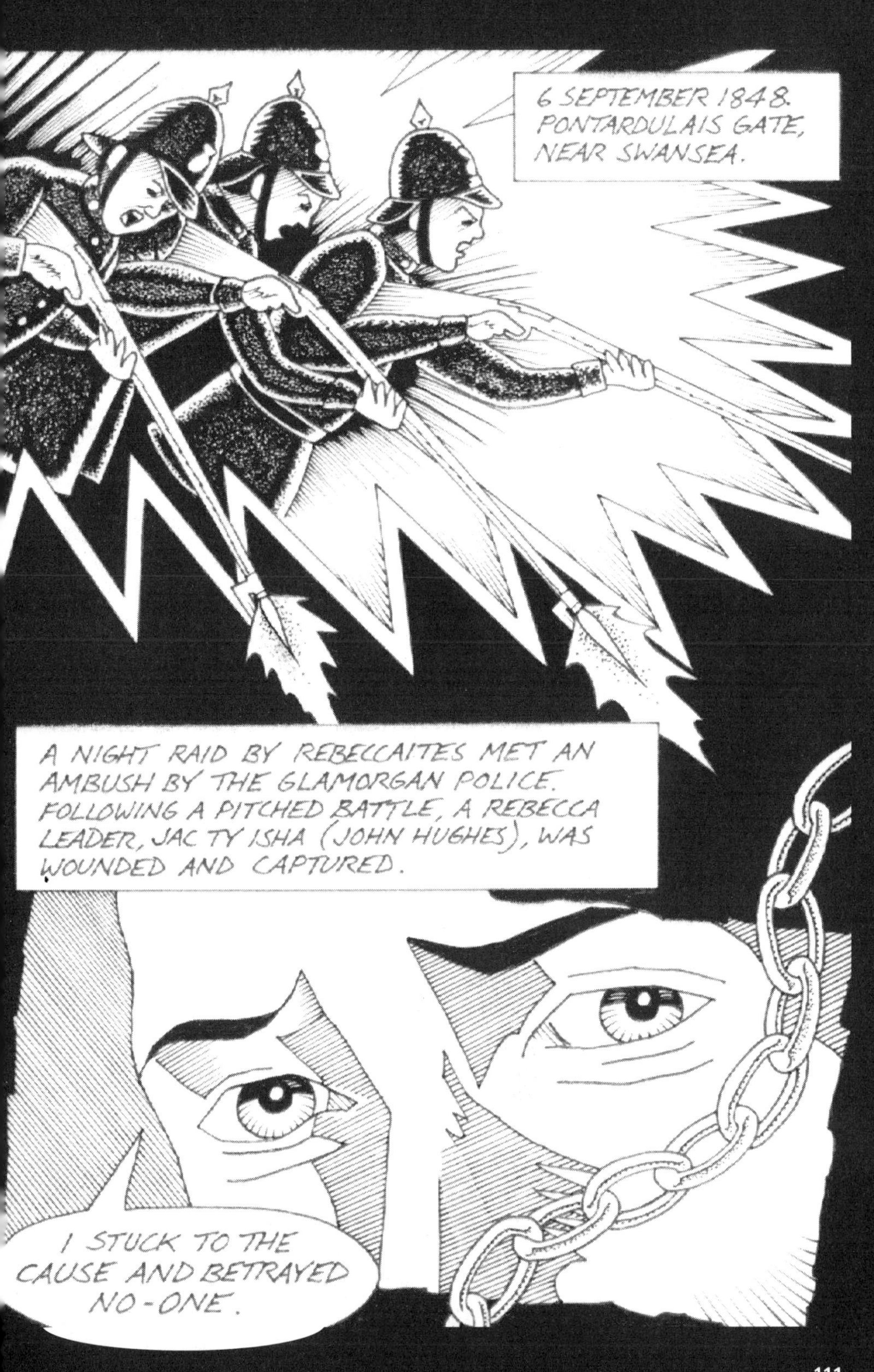
6 SEPTEMBER 1848. PONTARDULAIS GATE, NEAR SWANSEA.
A NIGHT RAID BY REBECCAITES MET AN AMBUSH BY THE GLAMORGAN POLICE. FOLLOWING A PITCHED BATTLE, A REBECCA LEADER, JAC TY ISHA (JOHN HUGHES), WAS WOUNDED AND CAPTURED.
I STUCK TO THE CAUSE AND BETRAYED NO-ONE.

AFTER FURTHER UNREST, TWO OTHER ORGANISERS WERE CAUGHT: SHONI SGUBOR FAWR ('JOHNNY BIG BARN', A BOXER) AND DAI'R CANTWR ('DAI THE SINGER', A POET).
DAI'R CANTWR'S POEMS, WRITTEN IN CARMARTHEN GAOL, BECAME HUGELY POPULAR. ALL THREE MEN WERE SENTENCED TO TRANSPORTATION FOR LIFE. REBECCAISM AFTERWARDS DECLINED, BUT THE TOLL SYSTEM WAS REVIEWED AND OTHER REFORMS INTRODUCED.

chapter eleven

IN THE NORTH, SMALL TENANT FARMERS, ALREADY STRUGGLING TO PAY RENT, HAD TO PAY TITHES TO THE ENGLISH CHURCH, EVEN THOUGH THE FARMFOLK THEMSELVES WERE WELSH NON-CONFORMIST. THEY REFUSED TO PAY THE TITHES IN 1887 AND SET UP AN ANTI-TITHE LEAGUE UNDER HOWELL GEE (SON OF ACTIVIST AND PUBLISHER THOMAS GEE).

ONE YOUNG LIBERAL WHO SUPPORTED THE TITHE REBELS WAS **TOM ELLIS**, WHO IN 1886 HAD FOUNDED THE NATIONALIST MOVEMENT **CYMRU FYDD** (YOUNG WALES), DEMANDING A SUBSTANTIAL DEGREE OF HOME RULE AND BECOMING A PROMINENT NATIONAL FORCE, WITH BRANCHES THROUGHOUT WALES.

ELLIS' CO-FOUNDER OF CYMRU FYDD, **DAVID LLOYD GEORGE** (1863-1945), TOOK UP THE STRUGGLE IN THE HOUSE OF COMMONS.

PROPOSALS IN PARLIAMENT FOR HOME RULE WERE REPEATEDLY DROPPED, AND LLOYD GEORGE LOST INTEREST IN THE MATTER. HE INTRODUCED CERTAIN SOCIAL REFORMS (E.G. OLD AGE PENSIONS, UNEMPLOYMENT INSURANCE, ETC.) AND BECAME PRIME MINISTER IN 1916. BUT AFTER THE FIRST WORLD WAR, MOUNTING UNEMPLOYMENT, INTERVENTION IN THE RUSSIAN CIVIL WAR AND USE OF THE 'BLACK AND TANS' IN IRELAND LOST HIM POPULAR SUPPORT.

AFTER 1908, LABOUR MINERS' MPs WERE VOTED INTO PARLIAMENT, AND TRADES UNIONS AND WORKING-CLASS VOTERS CAME TO LOOK TO LABOUR TO REPRESENT THEIR SPECIFIC INTERESTS. STILL, THERE REMAINED OVERALL WHOLEHEARTED SUPPORT FOR LLOYD GEORGE WHEN HE BECAME PRIME MINISTER, AND HIS WAR-TIME GOVERNMENT INCLUDED MANY PROMINENT WELSH LIBERALS. THE INFLUENCE OF WELSH LIBERALISM REMAINED APPARENT UNTIL AFTER THE WAR, WHEN LABOUR WERE SEEN TO HAVE A MORE POPULIST SOCIAL POLICY. DURING COALITION WITH THE CONSERVATIVES (1918-1922), THE LIBERALS STILL PUSHED THROUGH SOME REFORMS, SUCH AS THE HOUSING AND TOWN PLANNING ACT (1919), BUT AFTER 1922 IT WAS OBVIOUS THAT THE FUTURE LAY WITH THE LABOUR PARTY IN INDUSTRIAL WALES.
LLOYD GEORGE'S BIRTHPLACE IN LLANYSTUMDWY, NEAR CRICIETH, GWYNEDD, IS TODAY A MUSEUM.

THE REFORM ACTS 1832-84 INTRODUCED MANHOOD SUFFRAGE, GIVING THE WORKING MAN THE RIGHT TO VOTE.
BUT WOMEN REMAINED EXCLUDED.
WOMEN WOULD NOT GET THE RIGHT TO VOTE UNTIL AFTER THE FIRST WORLD WAR.
EVEN AFTER THAT, THERE WERE FEW WELSH WOMEN IN (UK) PARLIAMENT.
ONE MAN WHO DID SUPPORT EQUAL VOTING RIGHTS FOR WOMEN AND MEN WAS MICHAEL D. JONES, WHO LED A PARTY OF WELSH EMIGRANTS TO PATAGONIA IN 1865 TO ESTABLISH A WELSH-SPEAKING COMMUNITY ON EXPERIMENTAL DEMOCRATIC LINES, INCLUDING UNIVERSAL FRANCHISE. THEIR WELSH-SPEAKING ARGENTINIAN DESCENDANTS STILL LIVE THERE.

AN 1847 EDUCATIONAL REPORT ('THE 'BLUE BOOKS') CLAIMED THE WELSH LANGUAGE WAS INFERIOR, VULGAR AND BACKWARD. BANNED IN THE PLAYGROUND AS WELL AS THE CLASSROOM, ANY CHILD CAUGHT USING WELSH WAS PUNISHED WITH THE 'WELSH NOT' ROD.
WELSH NOT
SMAC !
SPEAK CIVILISED ENGLISH LIKE A GENTLEMAN, BOY !
WELSH IDENTITY FOUGHT BACK. IN 1856, EVAN AND JAMES JAMES COMPOSED 'MAE HEN WLAD FY NHADAU' (LAND OF MY FATHERS), WALES' NATIONAL ANTHEM.
FROM THE 1870'S ON, FEDERATED TRADES UNIONS WOULD FIGHT FOR EQUAL RIGHTS AND BETTER CONDITIONS FOR ALL.
THE TRADES UNION MOVEMENT IN WALES AT THIS TIME INCLUDED A 'RED DRAGON' MOVEMENT TO KEEP WELSH UNIONS INDEPENDENT.
IN PARLIAMENT, HOWEVER, IT WAS THE LIBERAL PARTY IN WHICH THE WELSH PEOPLE ENTRUSTED THEIR HOPES OF SOCIAL REFORM, HOME RULE AND CLASS EQUALITY.

A HAULIERS' STRIKE IN SOUTH WALES 1893-98, A BITTER CONFLICT INVOLVING THE USE OF TROOPS, CULMINATED IN THE FORMATION IN 1898 OF THE SOUTH WALES MINERS FEDERATION ('THE FED'), THE WELSH MINERS' OWN INDEPENDENT UNION.
SOUTH WALES MINERS FEDERATION
A STRIKE BY SLATE QUARRYMEN IN THE NORTH BEGAN AT BETHESDA QUARRIES IN 1900. THE OWNER, LORD PENRHYN, INDUSTRIALIST AND COUNTRY ARISTOCRAT, HAD CUT WAGES AND WORKING RIGHTS.
ONLY ENGLISHMEN OR HIGHLY FAVOURED, ENGLISH-SPEAKING WELSHMEN COULD BE MANAGERS.

PENRHYN ABSOLUTELY REFUSED TO NEGOTIATE. WHEN AT LAST THE STRIKERS SURRENDERED AND RETURNED TO WORK, HUNDREDS OF MEN WERE SACKED FOR THEIR PART IN THE STRIKE.

JAMES KEIR HARDIE (1856-1915), A SOCIALIST FROM SCOTLAND, FORMED THE INDEPENDENT LABOUR PARTY, FORERUNNER OF TODAY'S LABOUR PARTY.

I OFTEN WONDER WHY IT IS THAT SOME MEN OPPOSE HOME RULE FOR THE LAND OF THEIR BIRTH.
WHEN THE MEN ELECTED TO MAKE LAWS ARE BUT A SMALL PART OF A FOREIGN PARLIAMENT, THAT IS WHEN ALL NATIONAL FEELING DIES... I HAVE ALWAYS BEEN A STRONG SUPPORTER OF SELF-GOVERNMENT.
A STRIKE BY RAILWAYMEN ON THE TAFF VALE RAILWAY STIRRED THE TRADES UNION MOVEMENT INTO SPONSORING LABOUR MPs.
BRITAIN'S FIRST LABOUR MP, HARDIE BECAME MP FOR MERTHYR IN 1900. HE BOYCOTTED THE INVESTITURE OF THE PRINCE OF WALES IN 1911, REFUSING "TO COMMEMORATE ENGLAND'S SUPREMACY OVER THE WELSH".

SOUTH WALES, 1910. CAMBRIAN COLLIERIES LTD DECIDED TO CUT WAGES AND IMPOSE A LOCKOUT. 12,000 MINERS WENT ON STRIKE.
HARRIS'S
WHEN THE STRIKE LED TO RIOTING, THE STATE WAS SO ALARMED THAT WINSTON CHURCHILL (THEN HOME SECRETARY) SENT ARMED POLICE AND TROOPS INTO THE RHONDDA VALLEY.
CHURCHILL WAS NEVER QUITE FORGIVEN!

SOUTH WALES
ECHO
OFFICE
AT TONYPANDY ON NOVEMBER 21st 1910, HUSSARS CHARGED STRIKING MINERS WITH BAYONETS. COMMANDING OFFICER GENERAL MACREADY (LATER CHIEF OF THE NOTORIOUS 'BLACK AND TANS') ORDERED THE TROOPS TO FIRE ON THE DEMONSTRATORS.

TROOPS WERE ALSO SENT TO PONTYPRIDD TO OCCUPY THE TOWN AND MANY OTHER MINING COMMUNITIES WERE SIMILARLY BESIEGED DURING THE DISPUTE. SEVERAL PEOPLE WERE KILLED IN THE DISTURBANCES.
KING GEORGE V MEANWHILE ASKED AFTER THE HEALTH OF PIT PONIES!

THE STRIKE LASTED 10 MONTHS UNTIL THE MINERS WERE FORCED BACK TO WORK THROUGH THEIR FAMILIES' STARVATION.
A RESOLUTION AT THE 1911 I.L.P. ANNUAL CONFERENCE STATED "THERE IS NOTHING IN THE LABOUR AND SOCIALIST MOVEMENT WHICH IS HOSTILE TO THE BEST INTERESTS OF WELSH NATIONALISM", WHILE THEIR MAGAZINE 'Y GWLADGARWR CYMREIG' (THE WELSH PATRIOT) STRESSED THE IMPORTANCE OF HOME RULE.

Through Two World Wars

chapter twelve

TENSION BETWEEN EUROPE'S GREAT POWERS LED TO BRITAIN'S WAR WITH GERMANY IN 1914. OVER 280,000 WELSHMEN, MANY FRUSTRATED WITH POVERTY, MARCHED OFF TO FIGHT IN THE TRENCHES.

AAARGH!

WORLD WAR I (1914 – 1918)

RECRUITS WENT VOLUNTARILY AT FIRST, BELIEVING THE 'GREAT WAR' TO BE A WAR IN THE INTERESTS OF SMALL NATIONS. BUT THE REALITY AND WHOLESALE SLAUGHTER OF THE WAR BROUGHT DISILLUSION. CONSCRIPTION WAS INTRODUCED.

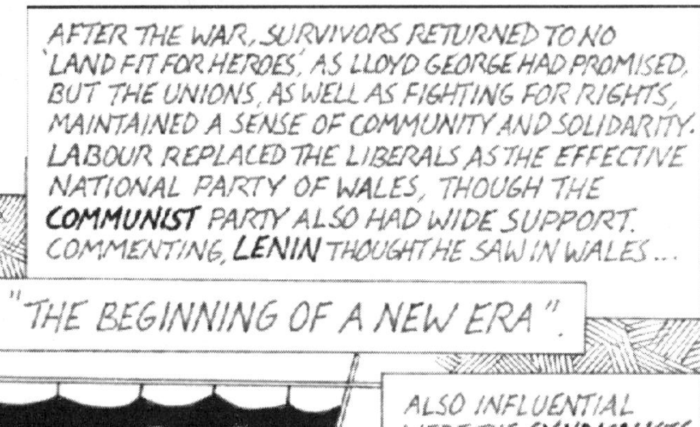
AFTER THE WAR, SURVIVORS RETURNED TO NO 'LAND FIT FOR HEROES,' AS LLOYD GEORGE HAD PROMISED, BUT THE UNIONS, AS WELL AS FIGHTING FOR RIGHTS, MAINTAINED A SENSE OF COMMUNITY AND SOLIDARITY. LABOUR REPLACED THE LIBERALS AS THE EFFECTIVE NATIONAL PARTY OF WALES, THOUGH THE **COMMUNIST** PARTY ALSO HAD WIDE SUPPORT. COMMENTING, **LENIN** THOUGHT HE SAW IN WALES...
"THE BEGINNING OF A NEW ERA".

S.O.S.
STRUGGLE OR STARVE
ALSO INFLUENTIAL WERE THE **SYNDICALISTS**, WHO STOOD FOR A DECENTRALISED, ANTI-AUTHORITARIAN FORM OF SOCIALISM AT COMMUNITY LEVEL, WHEREBY WORK-PLACES WOULD BE OWNED AND RUN BY WORKERS AND DEMOCRATIC UNIONS.

UP TO THE 1923 GENERAL ELECTION, THE LABOUR PARTY ACTIVELY AND STRONGLY SUPPORTED HOME RULE FOR WALES AS AN OFFICIAL POLICY AND A DEMOCRATIC NECESSITY. WELSH VOTES HELPED BRING LABOUR TO POWER IN 1923, BUT PRIME MINISTER RAMSAY MACDONALD WAS FORCED TO CONCEDE HIS POLICIES, FORMING A COALITION WITH THE CONSERVATIVES AND LIBERALS.
ISN'T LIFE A BITCH?
CAN A CHANGE OF BRITISH GOVERNMENT EVER CHANGE THE STATUS QUO?
AT PWLLHELI IN 1925, NATIONAL LIBERATIONIST SAUNDERS LEWIS FOUNDED PLAID CYMRU, THE WELSH NATIONALIST PARTY, TO CAMPAIGN FOR AN INDEPENDENT WELSH PARLIAMENT.

WHILE WORKERS' FAMILIES WONDERED WHERE THEIR NEXT MEAL WAS COMING FROM, MILLIONAIRES AND ARISTOCRATS CONTINUED TO LIVE IN LUXURY. AS A CONSEQUENCE, MANY COMMUNITIES – 'LITTLE MOSCOWS' – BECAME STRONGLY MILITANT OR COMMUNIST, TO THE HORROR OF THE PRESS IN FLEET STREET, AND A NUMBER OF WELSHMEN WENT OFF TO FIGHT AGAINST FASCISM IN THE SPANISH CIVIL WAR.

ONLY THROUGH REARMAMENT AND PREPARATION FOR WAR WAS THE ECONOMY RE-STABILISED. IN 1936, DURING SUCH WAR PREPARATIONS, THE GOVERNMENT DECIDED TO BUILD AN R.A.F. BOMBING SCHOOL. BUT THE QUESTION WAS: WHERE?

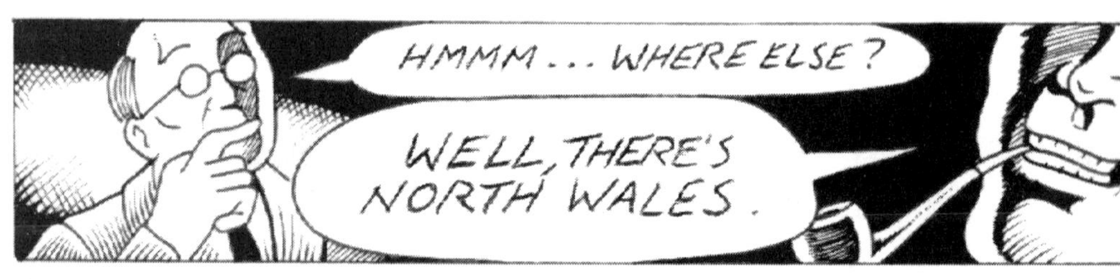

8th SEPTEMBER 1936. 1.30A.M. PLAID CYMRU MEMBERS SAUNDERS LEWIS, LEWIS VALENTINE AND D.J. WILLIAMS ATTACKED THE CENTRE (AT PENYBERTH, NEAR CRICIETH), SETTING FIRE TO BUILDINGS (NO PEOPLE WERE HARMED).

AT THEIR TRIAL AT CAERNARFON, THE WELSH JURY FAILED TO AGREE ON A VERDICT, AND PUBLIC SUPPORT WAS ENORMOUS. THE THREE WERE SENT TO LONDON FOR TRIAL AT THE OLD BAILEY, WHERE AN ENGLISH JURY FOUND THEM GUILTY. THEY WERE IMPRISONED IN WORMWOOD SCRUBBS.

THE LABOUR PARTY FORMED THE SOUTH WALES REGIONAL COUNCIL OF LABOUR IN 1937. THIS WOULD BECOME THE WELSH R.C.L. IN 1947 AND EVENTUALLY THE WALES LABOUR PARTY OF TODAY.

EUROPE'S POWERS WENT TO WAR AGAIN, AND ONCE MORE WALES WAS DRAWN IN.
WORLD WAR II (1939-1945)
WE'LL MEET AGAIN...
MANY TOWNS AND AREAS WERE BLITZED — 1000 CIVILIANS DIED IN 1941 ALONE — PARTICULARLY AT SWANSEA, WHERE A 3-DAY BLITZ DESTROYED THE TOWN. MEANWHILE IN PARLIAMENT, THE ISSUE OF HOME RULE AFTER THE WAR RE-EMERGED FOR REGULAR DEBATE.

AFTER THE WAR, A NEW ERA OF TECHNOLOGICAL AND ECONOMIC PROGRESS DID NOT REACH EXPECTATIONS.
MINISTRY MF OF FOOD
RATION BOOK
NO JAM TODAY AND NO JAM TOMORROW UNTIL WE'VE EARNED IT.
STAFFORD CRIPPS
WALES NEVER REACHED THE LEVEL OF PROSPERITY OF ENGLAND.
BESIDES, WHATEVER PROSPERITY EXISTED WAS MERELY TEMPORARY.
WALES
POST-WAR INDUSTRY
SUCCESSIVE BRITISH GOVERNMENTS FAILED TO MODERNISE WELSH INDUSTRY ADEQUATELY OR IN TIME.
WALES' OVER-DEPENDENCE ON TRADITIONAL HEAVY INDUSTRIES WOULD LEAD TO ITS DOWNFALL.
WE SHALL PLAN A NEW BRITAIN FROM LONDON!
PRIME MINISTER CLEMENT ATTLEE, WHO DURING THE WAR HAD SUPPORTED "COMPLETE AUTONOMY FOR WALES" IN RESPONSE TO THE WISHES OF HIS OWN PARTY IN WALES, NOW OPPOSED HOME RULE IN ANY FORM.

chapter thirteen

ANEURIN ('NYE') BEVAN (1897-1960), BORN IN TREDEGAR, GWENT, SON OF A WELSH-SPEAKING MINER (AND HIMSELF A MINERS' LEADER DURING THE 1926 STRIKE), BECAME A LEADING FIGURE IN THE POST-WAR LABOUR GOVERNMENT.

LIKE MOST OF HIS COMPATRIOTS, HE REMAINED FIRMLY MORE RADICAL THAN THE MAINSTREAM LEADERSHIP OF THE BRITISH LABOUR PARTY, YET HIS HANDS WERE TIED BY THE SYSTEM. UNABLE TO ABOLISH INJUSTICE OR INEQUALITY, HE DID HIS BEST TO ALLEVIATE IT, INTRODUCING REFORMS WHICH COULD BE REVERSED BY A LESS LIBERAL GOVERNMENT.

FOR EXAMPLE, HE INTRODUCED THE NATIONAL HEALTH SERVICE, FREQUENTLY UNDER ATTACK BY SUBSEQUENT CONSERVATIVE REGIMES.

AN ALL-PARTY 'PARLIAMENT FOR WALES' CAMPAIGN...

... AND THE FORWARDING OF A HOME RULE BILL BY LABOUR MP FOR MERTHYR S.O. DAVIES HELPED PUSH THE GOVERNMENT TO SET UP A WELSH OFFICE AND A SECRETARY OF STATE FOR WALES, THOUGH NO MEASURE OF ACTUAL HOME RULE WAS GRANTED YET.
DEMOCRATIC MASS ACTION (PASSIVE RESISTANCE) CAN EFFECTIVELY BRING ABOUT CHANGE. WHEN THIS FAILS, THE NEXT STAGE MAY BE ILLEGAL, NON-VIOLENT ACTION (CIVIL DISOBEDIENCE), BUT CONTINUAL FRUSTRATION OR SUPPRESSION OF DEMANDS HAS SOMETIMES (AS WITH THE PENYBERTH INCIDENT MENTIONED EARLIER) LED TO MORE VIOLENT ACTION.
IN 1952, LEFT-WING NATIONALISTS BLEW UP A WATER PIPELINE AT THE CLAERWEN DAM IN MID-WALES, WHICH SUPPLIED THE CITY OF BIRMINGHAM.
P-TOOM!
THEY TAKE OUR WATER, FLOOD OUR VALLEYS AND COMMUNITIES AND DESTROY OUR LANGUAGE AND HERITAGE.

STILL MORE SIGNIFICANT WAS THE DECISION BY LIVERPOOL CORPORATION IN 1955 TO BUILD THE TRYWERYN DAM IN MERIONETHSHIRE, FLOODING THE WELSH-SPEAKING VILLAGE OF CAPEL CELYN IN ORDER TO SUPPLY INDUSTRIAL WATER TO LIVERPOOL.

A WIDELY-SUPPORTED CAMPAIGN LED BY GWYNFOR EVANS WAS LAUNCHED, ONLY TO BE IGNORED BY THE STATE.

TWO YOUNG NATIONAL LIBERATIONISTS, DAI PRITCHARD AND DAI WALTERS ('THE 'BOYOS FROM GWENT') DRAINED OIL FROM THE ELECTRICAL TRANSFORMER ON THE SITE.

NEVERTHELESS, THE AUTHORITIES FLOODED THE VALLEY AND BUILT THE DAM AS PLANNED.

SUCH DESTRUCTIVE ATTACKS BY THE BRITISH AUTHORITIES ON WELSH LIFE AND LANGUAGE LED TO THE CREATION IN 1962 OF CYMDEITHAS YR IAITH GYMRAEG (WELSH LANGUAGE SOCIETY).
DETERMINED TO SAVE AND RESTORE THE WELSH LANGUAGE, CYMDEITHAS TURNED TO ILLEGAL (NOT 'TERRORIST') METHODS AFTER LEGAL PROTEST METHODS FAILED.
BYWYD I'R GYMRAEG
I THOUGHT THE WELSH WERE SUPPOSED TO BE A PEACEFUL PEOPLE!
ROGUES, BOLSHIES AND NE'ER-DO-WELLS THE LOT OF 'EM!
ROAD SIGNS IN ENGLISH WERE PAINTED OVER, SELECTED PROPERTY DAMAGED, TV TRANSMISSIONS SABOTAGED, AND DEMONSTRATIONS, SIT-INS AND OCCUPATION OF PUBLIC BUILDINGS HELD (DESPITE ARRESTS), DEMANDING PROPER STATUS FOR WELSH. CYMDEITHAS WOULD BECOME A MAJOR DYNAMIC FORCE, ACHIEVING MANY REFORMS.

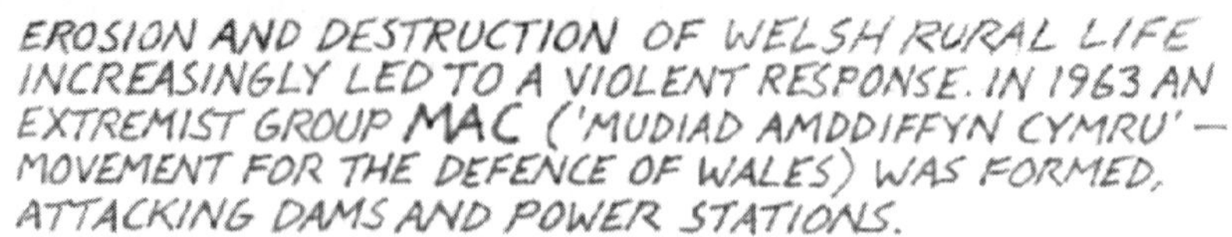

AFTER THEY TRIED TO INCITE THE PUBLIC TO VIOLENCE AT THE INVESTITURE OF THE PRINCE OF WALES AT CAERNARFON, 1969, THE LEADERS WERE JAILED.

BETWEEN 1980 AND 1982, 13 BOMB AND ARSON ATTACKS WERE CARRIED OUT ON ARMY RECRUITMENT OFFICES, CONSERVATIVE PARTY OFFICES AND STATE ESTABLISHMENTS BY THE 'WORKERS ARMY OF THE WELSH REPUBLIC' (**WAWR** = 'DAWN' IN WELSH).

AGAIN THERE WERE NO CASUALTIES, BUT THE AUTHORITIES CLAMPED DOWN SEVERELY. SPECIAL BRANCH LAID BLAME ON THE **WELSH SOCIALIST REPUBLICAN MOVEMENT** (FORMED 1979) AND LAUNCHED 'OPERATION FIRE', ROUNDING UP 52 OF WSRM'S 300 MEMBERS. AT THE 'CARDIFF EXPLOSIVES TRIAL' IN 1983, TWO PEOPLE WERE JAILED, BUT ABUSE OF POLICE POWERS BECAME APPARENT. INNOCENT WSRM MEMBERS WERE CLEARED, FIVE OF THEM HAVING BEEN HELD ON REMAND FOR UP TO TEN MONTHS.

IMPOSED DETERIORATION OF WELSH SOCIETY OCCURRED IN OTHER WAYS. THE 1960'S BROUGHT MORE AND MORE PIT CLOSURES AND BY 1966 MOST OF WALES WAS CLASSIFIED A 'DEVELOPMENT AREA' (i.e. INDUSTRIALLY BACKWARD), RELYING ON DIRECT CENTRAL GOVERNMENT ASSISTANCE.

CLOSED PITS WERE DANGEROUS. ON OCTOBER 21 1966, A DISUSED SLAG HEAP AVALANCHED OVER PART OF THE VILLAGE OF ABERFAN, COVERING THE LOCAL SCHOOL. 144 PEOPLE DIED, INCLUDING 111 CHILDREN.

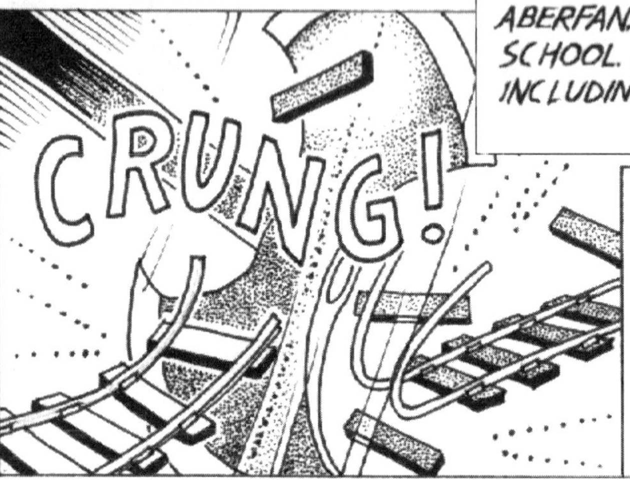

MEANWHILE, THE 'BEECHING AXE' FELL, CLOSING ALMOST HALF OF WALES' RAILWAY LINES.

(RICHARD BEECHING WAS CHAIRMAN OF THE BRITISH RAILWAYS BOARD 1963-65).

TEMPORARY INDUSTRIAL PROGRESS PROVED TO BE 'TOO LITTLE, TOO LATE'. WITH THE CLOSURE OF THE STEELWORKS AT EBBW VALE AND EAST MOORS IN THE MID 1970'S, IT WAS CLEAR THAT A CRISIS UNSEEN SINCE THE 1930'S WAS NOW BEFALLING WALES.

BY THE LATE 1960'S, CAMPAIGNING BY CYMDEITHAS RESULTED IN THE INTRODUCTION OF THE **WELSH LANGUAGE ACT**,* GRANTING EQUAL STATUS TO WELSH FOR ALL PURPOSES, INCLUDING OFFICIAL, LEGAL AND EDUCATIONAL.

OTHER MILITANT WELSH LANGUAGE GROUPS SUCH AS **ADFER** ('RESTORATION' IN WELSH) HAD BY NOW EMERGED, AND MANY HAD COME TO ASSOCIATE THE LANGUAGE WITH REVOLUTION AS WELL AS REFORM.

DUE TO A RISE OF NATIONALISM, JIM CALLAGHAN'S GOVERNMENT OFFERED 'DEVOLUTION' – A DEGREE OF SELF-ADMINISTRATION THROUGH A WELSH ASSEMBLY.

THE ASSEMBLY WOULD ONLY HAVE ADMINISTRATIVE, NOT IMPORTANT DECISION-MAKING POWERS. IN A REFERENDUM IN 1979 THE WELSH PEOPLE, DISCOURAGED, DISILLUSIONED AND SCEPTICAL, LARGELY ABSTAINED OR VOTED AGAINST THE TOKEN ASSEMBLY AND THE MATTER WAS DROPPED.

DEVOLUTION DELAYED

chapter fourteen

THEN, OUT OF THE GENERAL ELECTION OF 1979, CAME THE MOST CRUSHING BLOW TO WALES IN MODERN TIMES...

DESPITE THE EXPRESS WISHES OF THE MAJORITY OF WELSH PEOPLE, MARGARET THATCHER WAS VOTED INTO POWER.

THOUGH WALES HAD VOTED ANTI-TORY, IT WAS TO GET A TORY GOVERNMENT – AND FACE THE PUNISHMENT.

THATCHER'S ATTITUDE WAS PATRONISING AND DICTATORIAL. IMMEDIATELY ATTACKING PUBLIC SERVICES, SHE CUT SCHOOL AND HOSPITAL PROVISIONS, CLOSED PREMISES DOWN AND CURBED WELFARE BENEFITS, REVERSING REFORMS INTRODUCED BY PREVIOUS GOVERNMENTS. THE EFFORTS OF LLOYD GEORGE AND NYE BEVAN WERE FOR NOTHING. PUBLIC MONEY WAS SPENT INSTEAD ON ARMAMENTS AND WEAPONS OF WAR.

WHILE UNEMPLOYMENT SOARED TO DESPAIRING LEVELS, THE ECONOMY CONTINUED TO DECLINE, DESPITE HOLLOW PROMISES OF RECOVERY. TRADES UNION AND EMPLOYMENT RIGHTS WERE CRUSHED AND CIVIL LIBERTIES ATTACKED.

THATCHER PREACHED 'FREE ENTERPRISE' BUT, IN AN INCREASINGLY COMPETITIVE SOCIETY, MOST SMALL BUSINESSES FOUND IT HARD TO COMPETE. LIFE BECAME EASIER FOR THE RICH AND INCREASINGLY TOUGH FOR THE UNDERPRIVILEGED.

AS COUNCIL HOUSE BUILDING AND MAINTENANCE ALL BUT CAME TO A STOP THROUGH LACK OF GOVERNMENT FUNDING, A SERIOUS HOUSING PROBLEM EMERGED THROUGHOUT WALES. IN RURAL NORTH WALES, THE SITUATION TURNED UGLY. RESENTMENT TOWARDS ABSENTEE OWNERS, WHO BOUGHT RURAL HOUSES FOR USE AS HOLIDAY COTTAGES, LED TO VIOLENCE.

OVER THE NEXT TEN YEARS, AT LEAST 130 ATTACKS BY THE **'MEIBION GLYNDŴR'** OCCURRED (THE HOUSES WERE ENSURED UNOCCUPIED AT THE TIME OF ATTACK – NO PEOPLE WERE HARMED).
EVENTUALLY, NOT ONLY THE HOLIDAY HOMES, BUT ESTATE AGENTS' OFFICES IN LONDON, CHESTER AND ELSEWHERE WHICH SOLD THE HOUSES WERE ATTACKED.

MEANWHILE, DEMANDS FOR A SEPARATE WELSH TELEVISION CHANNEL WERE IGNORED BY THE GOVERNMENT UNTIL MASS PROTESTS AND A TV LICENCE STRIKE BROKE OUT.
PLAID CYMRU LEADER GWYNFOR EVANS BEGAN A HUNGER STRIKE AND THE GOVERNMENT BACKED DOWN. SIANEL 4 CYMRU WAS LAUNCHED IN 1982.

BRITAIN BEGAN TO IMPORT FOREIGN COAL FROM COUNTRIES WITH OPPRESSIVE REGIMES SUCH AS SOUTH AFRICA AND COLOMBIA. THE FOREIGN COAL WAS CHEAPER IN THE SHORT TERM, BUT WOULD LATER PROVE A DANGER TO THE ENVIRONMENT AND A FALSE ECONOMY.

THE MINERS OF WALES JOINED THE NATIONAL MINERS' STRIKE OF 1984-85 TO FIGHT PIT CLOSURES.
THE STRIKE WAS BEATEN AND - WITH ONLY 3 EXCEPTIONS - ALL COAL MINES IN WALES CLOSED DOWN. WALES MOURNED THE DEATH OF THE RHONDDA AND OTHER COMMUNITIES AS THE NATION BECAME AN ECONOMIC WASTELAND OF UNEMPLOYMENT.

ACTIVISTS FROM THE MINERS' STRIKE JOINED WITH W.S.R.M. AROUND THEIR MAGAZINE 'Y FANER GOCH' IN OCTOBER 1986 TO FORM CYMRU GOCH, WHICH WENT ON TO PLACE BOROUGH COUNCILLORS IN BEDLINOG AND TRELEWIS AND TO CONTROL THE AREA'S COMMUNITY COUNCIL. CYMRU GOCH AIM FOR A WELSH SOCIALIST REPUBLIC.

JOHN MAJOR, WHO HAD REPLACED THATCHER IN 1990 AS PRIME MINISTER, REMAINED IN POWER. HE IMPLEMENTED THATCHER'S POLL TAX, AN UNFAIR AND WIDELY-HATED LOCAL TAXING SYSTEM WHICH CAUSED OUTRAGE AND WIDESPREAD PROTEST.
WELCOME TO THE CARING NINETIES.
DEMOCRATIAETH I GYMRU!
HE CONTINUED TO IMPOSE UNWANTED HARD-LINE POLICIES ON WALES, CLOSING MORE STEELWORKS AND THREATENING MORE PIT CLOSURES.

WALES' 'BOOM-OR-BUST' ECONOMY CAME OF HAVING AN ECONOMY OWNED AND CONTROLLED FROM OUTSIDE. WHILE LONDON AND FOREIGN MULTINATIONAL COMPANIES — 'INVESTORS' — MADE A PROFIT FROM WALES, SMALLER LOCAL FIRMS OR COOPERATIVES WERE UNABLE TO COMPETE. THE TORY DREAM OF 'ENTERPRISE INITIATIVE' HAD FAILED IN WALES.

WHOLE INDUSTRIES WERE CLOSED DOWN AND THE NATIONALISED ONES SOLD OFF TO PRIVATE OWNERSHIP, WHILE WALES HAD NO SAY IN THE DEGREE OR FORM OF PUBLIC OWNERSHIP ITS PEOPLE WANT, NOR AN INDEPENDENT VOICE ON E.C. MATTERS.

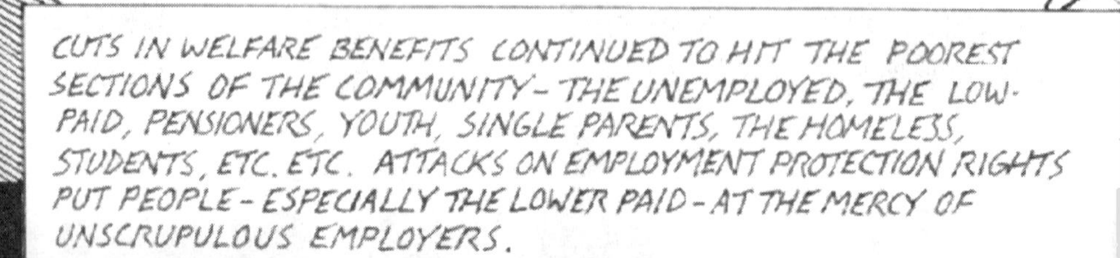

CUTS IN WELFARE BENEFITS CONTINUED TO HIT THE POOREST SECTIONS OF THE COMMUNITY – THE UNEMPLOYED, THE LOW-PAID, PENSIONERS, YOUTH, SINGLE PARENTS, THE HOMELESS, STUDENTS, ETC. ETC. ATTACKS ON EMPLOYMENT PROTECTION RIGHTS PUT PEOPLE – ESPECIALLY THE LOWER PAID – AT THE MERCY OF UNSCRUPULOUS EMPLOYERS.

WALES HAD LONG SUFFERED FROM INADEQUATE HOUSING. THE THATCHER-MAJOR ADMINISTRATION VIRTUALLY BROUGHT COUNCIL HOUSING TO A STOP, WHILE REPOSSESSION OF 'PRIVATE' HOUSING MORE THAN DOUBLED WITHIN TWO YEARS OF MAJOR'S COMING TO POWER. WITH HOMELESSNESS IN WALES A SERIOUS AND RISING PROBLEM, MANY WELSH PEOPLE WENT TO LONDON TO LOOK FOR WORK, ONLY TO FIND HOMELESSNESS AND DESTITUTION THERE.

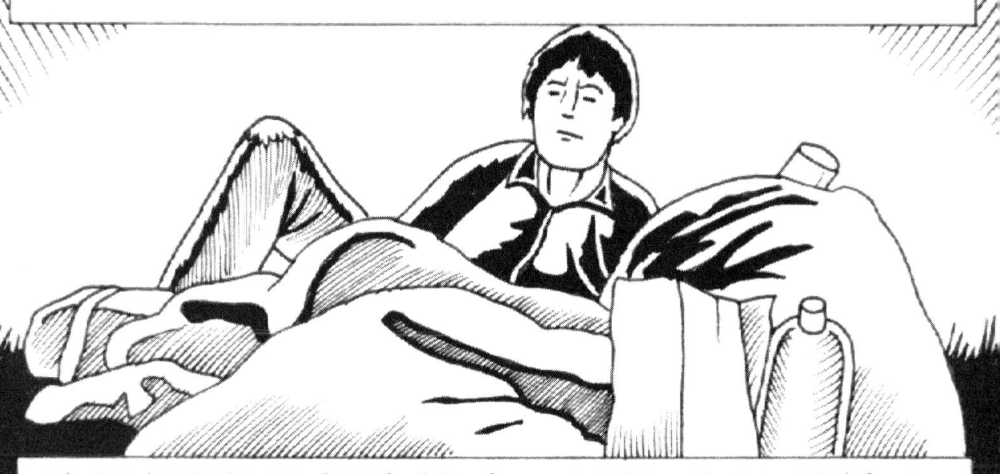

IN THE ABSENCE OF SOCIO-POLITICAL AWARENESS, FRUSTRATION CAN LEAD TO CRIME, AND WALES' CRIME RATE IN DEPRIVED AREAS REFLECTED HOPELESS SOCIAL CONDITIONS.

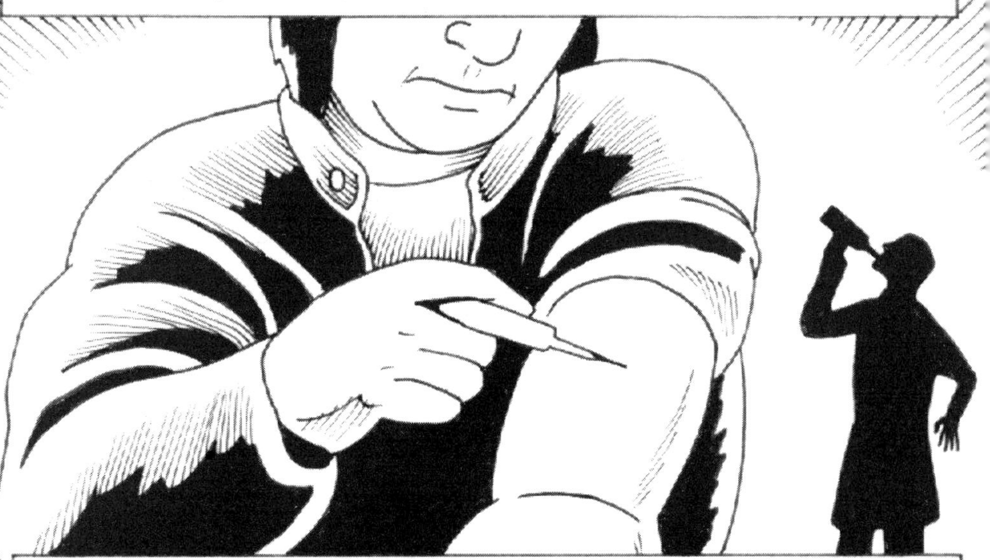

DRUG AND ALCOHOL ABUSE WERE A SERIOUS PROBLEM, AND WALES SUFFERED FROM A POOR HEALTH RECORD GENERALLY, A SITUATION WORSENED BY THE DRASTIC CUTBACKS SUFFERED BY THE HEALTH, HOSPITAL AND DISABILITY SERVICES.

EDUCATION SIMILARLY SUFFERED, WITH SCHOOLS UNDERSTAFFED AND UNDEREQUIPPED. WALES HAD NO SEPARATE EDUCATION SYSTEM FROM ENGLAND, WITH EDUCATIONAL MATTERS DICTATED FROM LONDON.
AR GAU
SCHOOL
CLOSED
CLOSED
BUT MANY OF THOSE SOCIAL PROBLEMS AREN'T JUST WELSH PROBLEMS. CERTAIN OTHER REGIONS OF BRITAIN SUFFER SIMILAR CONDITIONS.
WALES IS NOT A REGION IT IS A NATION!

ALL THINGS CONSIDERED, WALES WAS IN A STATE OF CRISIS.
IT'S TIME FOR CHANGE!
BUT THE SITUATION WAS UNLIKELY TO IMPROVE UNDER THE SYSTEM.
UNDER WESTMINSTER DOMINATION, WALES WOULD REMAIN A MINORITY, PERIPHERAL REGION WITH DEPENDENT OR SUBORDINATE STATUS.
THERE WAS, OF COURSE, A WAY OUT!

ANTI-TORY PARTIES IN WALES SUPPORTED HOME RULE OR SELF-GOVERNMENT TO SOME EXTENT.

THOUGH DISAGREEING ON THE DEGREE OR FORM THAT HOME RULE SHOULD TAKE, THEY SHOWED UNITY IN THEIR MUTUAL SUPPORT FOR AN EFFECTIVE WELSH ASSEMBLY OR PARLIAMENT.

BUT WOULD THE PEOPLE?

chapter 15

AFTER THE RESIGNATION OF NEIL KINNOCK, JOHN SMITH BECAME LEADER OF THE OPPOSITION IN THE UK PARLIAMENT. WHEN HE DIED OF A SUDDEN HEART ATTACK IN 1994, HE WAS REPLACED BY TONY BLAIR, WHO REFORMED 'NEW LABOUR', TAKING A MORE 'PRAGMATIC' APPROACH TO ECONOMIC AND SOCIAL POLICY – MUCH LESS RADICAL THAN LABOUR HAD TRADITIONALLY STOOD FOR. IT WAS HOPED BY THE PARTY THAT THE NEW STANCE WOULD APPEAL TO VOTERS IN THE ENGLISH HOME COUNTIES, MAKING IT ELECTABLE.

NEW LABOUR PROMISED TO HOLD A REFERENDUM ON WELSH HOME RULE WITHIN A YEAR OF TAKING OFFICE, AND TO ACTIVELY ENCOURAGE SUPPORT FOR A WELSH ASSEMBLY.

THE MODERATION OF LABOUR'S POLICIES HAD THE DESIRED EFFECT. IN THE GENERAL ELECTION OF 1997, THEY WON A LANDSLIDE VICTORY OVER THE TORY GOVERNMENT. THE LONG YEARS OF CONSERVATIVE RULE (UNWANTED BY MOST WELSH) WERE OVER.
ON BECOMING PRIME MINISTER, BLAIR KEPT HIS WORD ON THE REFERENDUM.
DEVOLUTION
PLANS FOR A WELSH ASSEMBLY
HUH! THIS WILL BREAK UP THE UNITED KINGDOM!

ON 12TH SEPTEMBER 1997, THE REFERENDUM WAS PUT TO THE PEOPLE OF WALES, ASKING THEM TO CHOOSE WHETHER OR NOT THEY WANTED A WELSH ASSEMBLY.

AS THE RESULTS WERE RETURNED FOR COUNTING THAT NIGHT, THE SITUATION BEGAN TO LOOK GLOOMY FOR SUPPORTERS OF THE ASSEMBLY, AS THEIR VOTES BECAME WELL OUTWEIGHED BY VOTES AGAINST IT.

THEN, WHEN IT SEEMED THAT ALL WAS LOST, THE RESULTS FOR THE LAST CONSTITUENCY, CARMARTHENSHIRE, CAME IN. THE BALANCE WAS SUDDENLY TIPPED!

OVERWHELMINGLY IN FAVOUR OF HOME RULE, THE DECISIVE CARMARTHENSHIRE VOTES WERE ENOUGH TO SECURE AN EXTREMELY NARROW OVERALL MAJORITY IN FAVOUR OF THE ASSEMBLY.

RON DAVIES

THE THEN SECRETARY OF STATE FOR WALES, RON DAVIES, OVERSEEING THE REFERENDUM, WAS JUBILANT, AS WERE MANY LABOUR SUPPORTERS AND NATIONALISTS.

THAT'S THE SPIRIT!
YES
YES
YES
YES
YES
YES
YES
WELSH ASSEMBLY
REFERENDUM
OWAIN GLYNDŴR
THE RESULT OF THE REFERENDUM WAS CRUCIAL AS IT MEANT THAT, FROM THIS POINT ONWARDS, THE PEOPLE OF WALES WOULD BE ABLE TO CHOOSE THEIR OWN DESTINY AS WELL AS CONTROL THEIR OWN INTERNAL AFFAIRS. IT WAS, INDEED, THE BIGGEST TURNING POINT IN WALES' HISTORY SINCE ITS ANNEXATION BY ENGLAND. WALES' NEAREST APPROACH TO A WELSH PARLIAMENT, FOR THE FIRST TIME SINCE THE DAYS OF OWAIN GLYNDŴR, WOULD BECOME A REALITY.

ON 19TH NOVEMBER 1998 THE UK PARLIAMENT PASSED THE GOVERNMENT OF WALES ACT, MAKING A DEVOLVED WELSH ASSEMBLY LEGAL AND CONSTITUTIONAL, GUARANTEED BY LAW. THE ESTABLISHMENT OF THE ASSEMBLY WAS TO BE OVERSEEN BY ALUN MICHAEL, WHO REPLACED RON DAVIES AS WELSH SECRETARY AFTER THE LATTER'S RESIGNATION FOLLOWING AN EMBARRASSING INCIDENT.

WHILE THE NEW ASSEMBLY BUILDING WAS BEING BUILT IN THE FORMER DOCKLANDS OF CARDIFF, TEMPORARY PREMISES HAD TO BE FOUND. CARDIFF'S CRICKHOWELL HOUSE WAS SELECTED FOR THIS PURPOSE, AND IT WAS HERE THAT THE ASSEMBLY WOULD BE OFFICIALLY OPENED IN 1999.

THE ASSEMBLY THUS HOUSED, PLANS WERE THOUGHT OUT AS TO HOW IT WOULD WORK.

IT WAS DECIDED THAT IT SHOULD OPERATE PARTLY ON A 'FIRST-PAST-THE-POST' SYSTEM (LIKE THE UK PARLIAMENT) AND PARTLY BY PROPORTIONAL REPRESENTATION (PR).

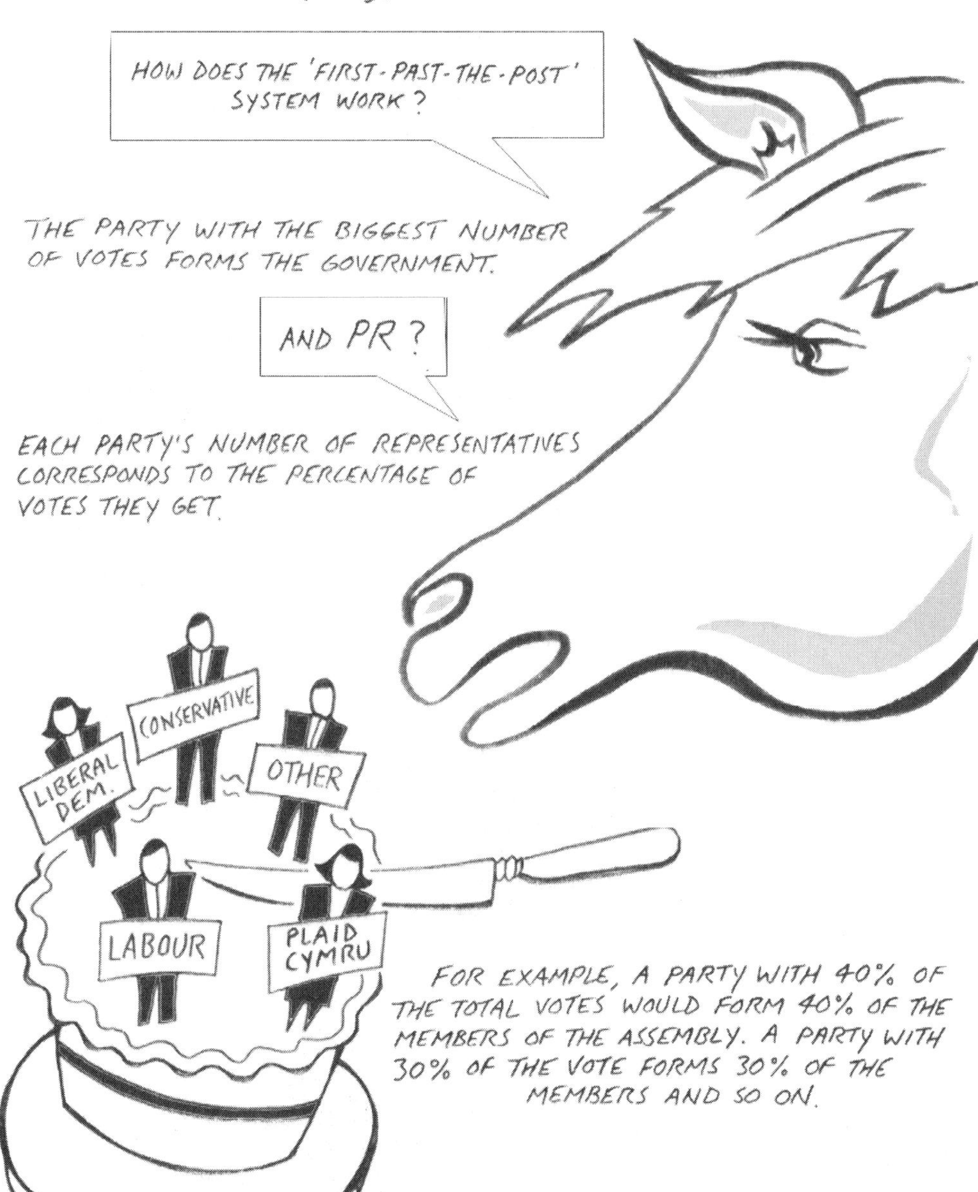

28th MAY 1999
The opening of the

WELSH ASSEMBLY,

CHALLENGES REMAIN FOR THE WELSH ASSEMBLY...

UNEMPLOYMENT, HOMELESSNESS, POVERTY AND UNDERFUNDING OF PUBLIC SERVICES REMAIN PROBLEMS TO BE OVERCOME AND, SINCE THE WELSH ASSEMBLY CANNOT MAKE LAWS OR CONSTITUTIONAL CHANGES WITHOUT THE APPROVAL OF CENTRAL GOVERNMENT IN LONDON, WESTMINSTER CONTROL PUTS RESTRAINT ON WELSH ACTION.

NOR DOES THE WELSH ASSEMBLY HAVE ECONOMIC CONTROL.
WITH MANY OF ITS LARGEST COMPANIES BASED IN LONDON OR ELSEWHERE, WALES' ECONOMY IS EFFECTIVELY CONTROLLED FROM OUTSIDE.
THE ASSEMBLY, HAVING NO POWERS OF TAXATION,* IS UNABLE TO RAISE REVENUE.
*UNLIKE THE SCOTTISH PARLIAMENT

AT THE TIME OF THE LEGISLATION OF THE WELSH ASSEMBLY, THERE WERE ONLY 4 WOMEN AMONG 38 WELSH MPs IN A UK PARLIAMENT OF 650. THE ASSEMBLY HOPES TO ADDRESS SUCH INEQUALITY, LOOKING ULTIMATELY TOWARDS AN EQUAL BALANCE OF THE SEXES AMONG ITS MEMBERS.

IT IS HOPED THAT RACIAL INEQUALITY WILL ALSO BE TACKLED, WITH GREATER REPRESENTATION FOR ETHNIC MINORITY GROUPS IN THE ASSEMBLY. FOR WELSH NATIONAL AWARENESS IS A CIVIC, NOT A RACIAL, ISSUE.
ANYONE LIVING PERMANENTLY IN WALES, REGARDLESS OF THEIR BIRTHPLACE OR ETHNIC ORIGIN, MAY CONSIDER THEMSELVES WELSH.

INCOMERS BORN OUTSIDE WALES HAVE CONTRIBUTED TO WELSH AFFAIRS OR CULTURE, WHILE WELSH-BORN PEOPLE OF RACIAL MINORITY BACKGROUND HAVE HELPED PUT WALES ON THE MAP.

WALES' ENVIRONMENT SUFFERS FROM POLLUTION, LARGELY FROM THE ENGLISH MIDLANDS. AFTER THATCHER CLOSED THE WELSH COAL MINES TO IMPORT CHEAP FOREIGN COAL, IT TRANSPIRED THAT THE IMPORTED COAL HAD A HIGH SULPHURIC CONTENT. AS A RESULT, INDUSTRY POURS TOXIC SMOKE INTO THE AIR AND WALES' ONCE PRISTINE LAKES AND RIVERS ARE CONTAMINATED WITH ACID RAIN. NUCLEAR POWER POSES ANOTHER THREAT THROUGH POTENTIAL DANGER OF MELTDOWN OR LEAKAGE.

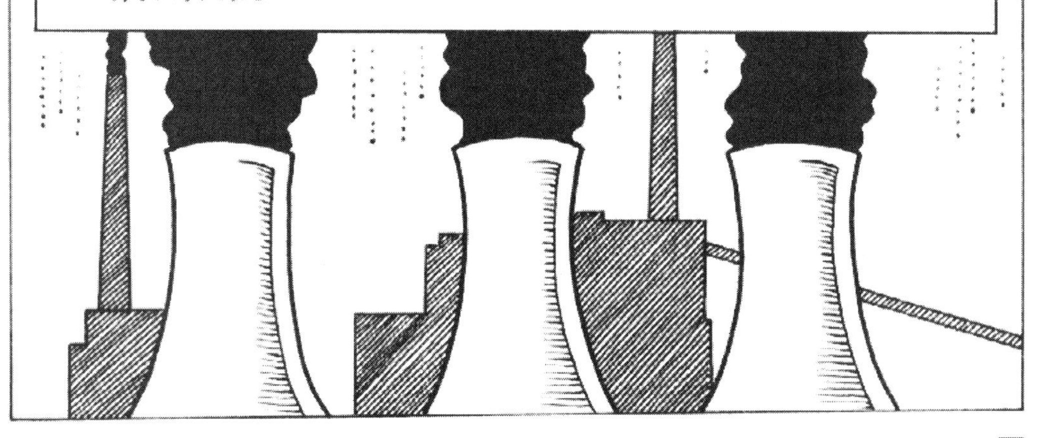

WALES HAS NO CONTROL OVER ITS OWN DEFENCE MATTERS, AND IS THEREFORE IMPLICITLY INVOLVED IN BRITAIN'S WARS IN OTHER PARTS OF THE WORLD (DURING THE FALKLANDS WAR OF 1982, WELSHMEN ACTUALLY FOUGHT WELSH-SPEAKING ARGENTINIANS!). MEANWHILE, THE R.A.F. PRACTICE WARGAMES OVER THE COUNTRYSIDE.

IN 1982 WALES BECAME EUROPE'S FIRST 'NUCLEAR FREE' COUNTRY AFTER ALL ITS COUNTY COUNCILS AGREED TO BAN NUCLEAR WEAPONS. NEVERTHELESS, THE ROYAL ORDNANCE FACTORY AT LLANISHEN, CARDIFF, CONTINUED TO MAKE CASINGS FOR NUCLEAR BOMBS. A 'NUCLEAR FREE' POLICY WILL NOT EXCLUDE WALES AS A POTENTIAL TARGET IN THE EVENT OF BRITAIN BEING INVOLVED IN NUCLEAR WAR.

THE WELSH LANGUAGE IS IN A CRITICAL STATE. ORIGINALLY SPOKEN THROUGHOUT ALL OF WALES (AND EVEN BEYOND), AND STILL THE LANGUAGE OF 90% OF THE POPULATION IN THE LAST CENTURY, IT IS NOW SPOKEN BY ONLY 20% OF THE WELSH PEOPLE. THE ACTIONS OF CYMDEITHAS HAVE BROUGHT ABOUT SUBSTANTIAL REFORMS, BUT CAMPAIGNING WILL CONTINUE FOR THE REVIVAL OF WELSH.

BUT NOW THAT THE PEOPLE OF WALES HAVE THEIR OWN ASSEMBLY, ALL THESE AND OTHER ISSUES CAN BE DEBATED ON WELSH SOIL.
FURTHERMORE, WE ARE ABLE AT LAST TO CHOOSE OUR OWN DESTINY!

WALES' NATIONALITY HAS SURVIVED AGAINST ALL THE ODDS BECAUSE THE NATION HAS KEPT ITS SOUL.
AND SHOULD ITS PEOPLE WISH TO TAKE THINGS FURTHER...
...THEN THAT IS A DECISION WE ALONE MUST TAKE.
THROUGH TIME, THE ASSEMBLY MAY BE UPGRADED TO A PARLIAMENT, WITH GREATER POWERS AND A GREATER LEVEL OF SELF-GOVERNMENT.
ONLY THE PEOPLE OF WALES CAN DECIDE ON HOW FAR THEY WISH TO GO. THE FUTURE OF WALES IS IN ITS OWN PEOPLE'S HANDS.

A NEW WALES IS AWAKENING!

Royal Houses of Wales

Kings who united the whole–or most–of Wales are shown in **BOLD CAPITALS**

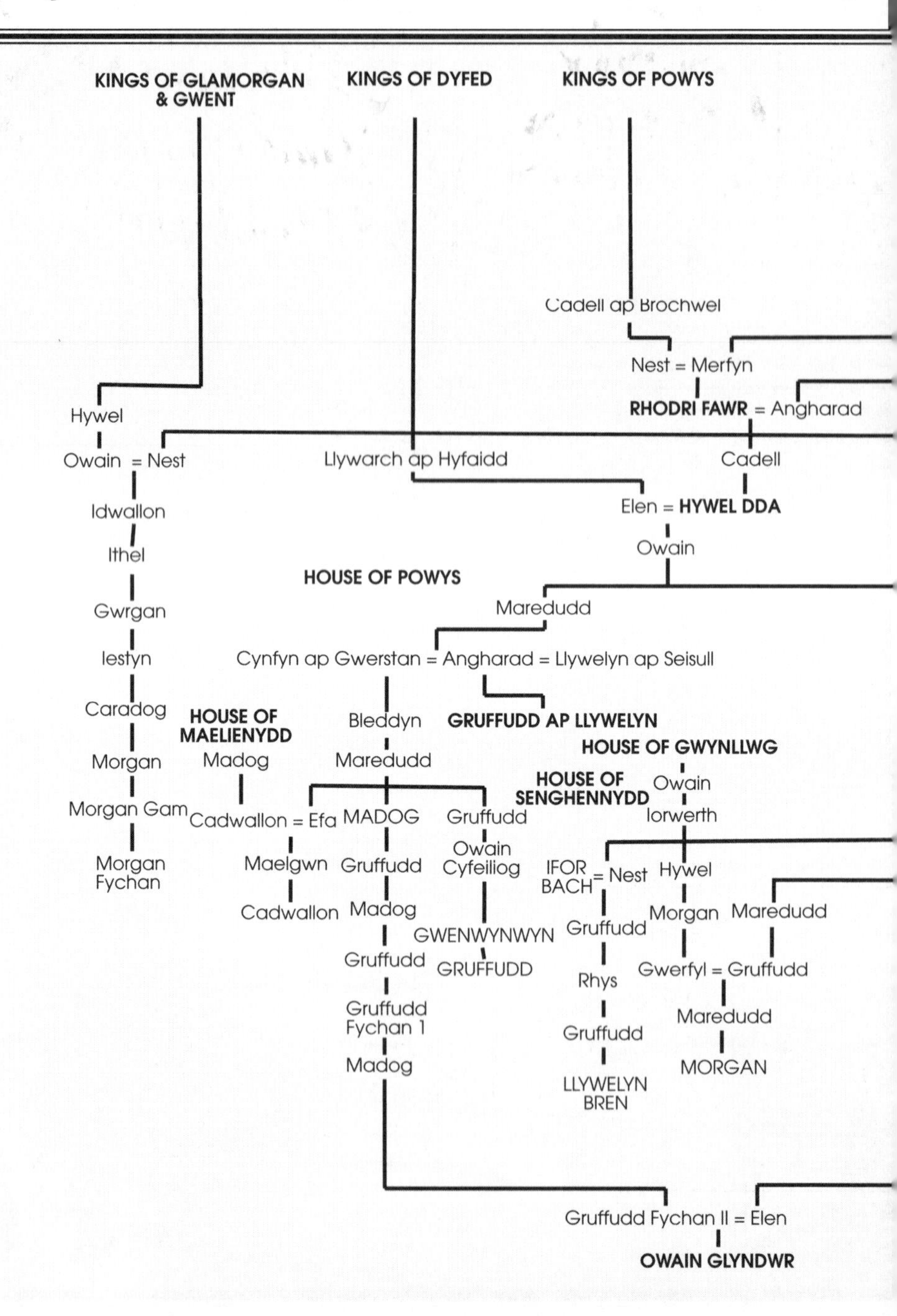

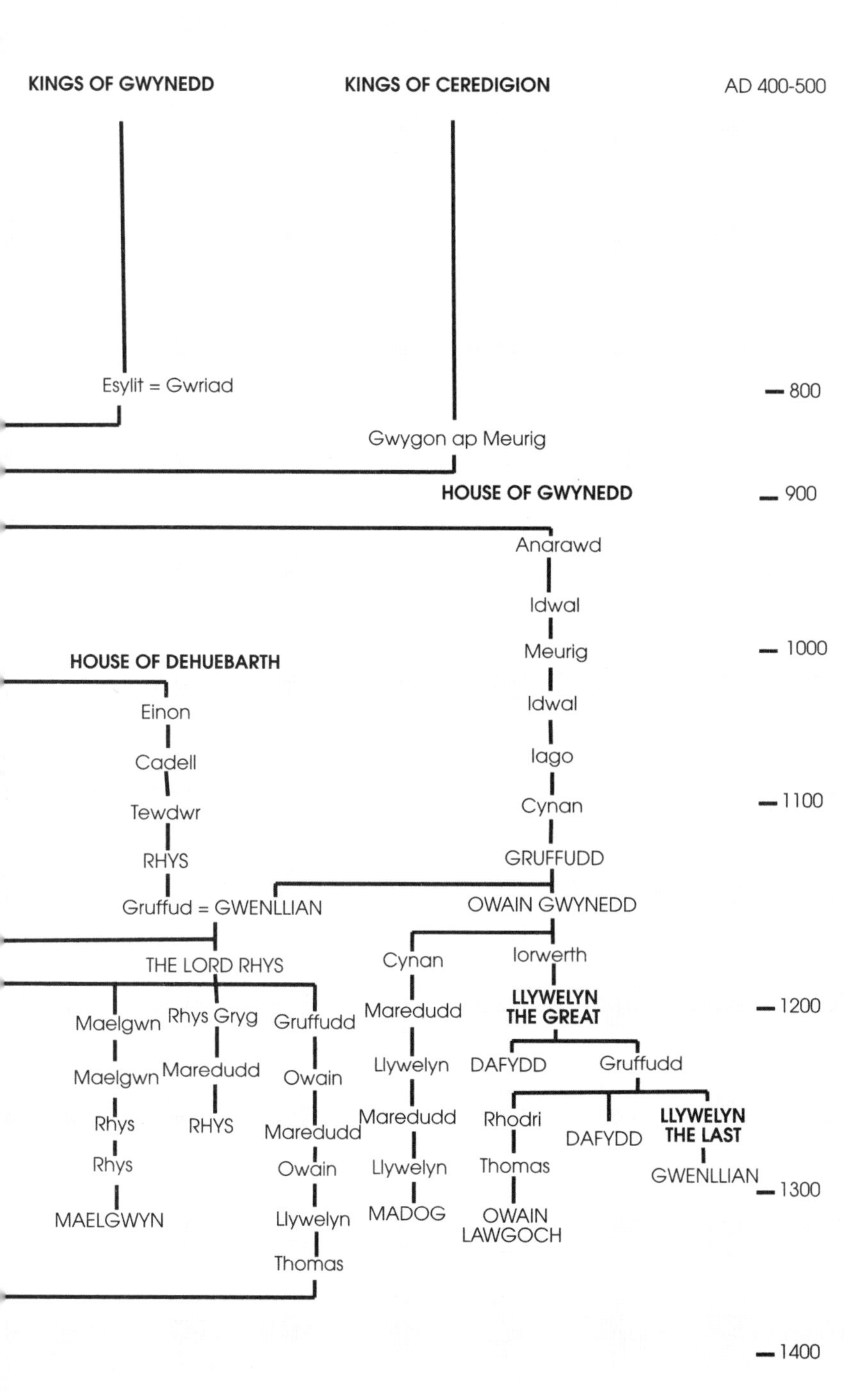
KINGS OF GWYNEDD
KINGS OF CEREDIGION
AD 400-500
Esylit = Gwriad
800
Gwygon ap Meurig
HOUSE OF GWYNEDD
900
Anarawd
Idwal
Meurig
1000
HOUSE OF DEHUEBARTH
Idwal
Einon
Iago
Cadell
Tewdwr
Cynan
1100
RHYS
GRUFFUDD
Gruffud = GWENLLIAN
OWAIN GWYNEDD
THE LORD RHYS
Cynan
Iorwerth
LLYWELYN
THE GREAT
1200
Maelgwn
Rhys Gryg
Gruffudd
Maredudd
Maelgwn
Maredudd
Owain
Llywelyn
DAFYDD
Gruffudd
Rhys
RHYS
Maredudd
Maredudd
Rhodri
DAFYDD
LLYWELYN
THE LAST
Rhys
Owain
Llywelyn
Thomas
GWENLLIAN
1300
MAELGWYN
Llywelyn
MADOG
OWAIN
LAWGOCH
Thomas
1400

chronology

500 - 100 BC	Celts arrive in Cymru/Wales.
AD 43	Romans arrive in Britain.
AD 51	Celtic leader Caradog defeated by Romans.
AD 78	Wales (Cambria) finally conquered by Romans.
410	Romans withdraw. Dark Ages begin.
c.500	Celts, possibly led by legendary Arthur, defeat Saxons at Mount Badon.
500-550	Celtic saints bring Christianity to Wales.
c.770	Saxon king Offa of Mercia orders construction of Offa's Dyke, forming Welsh-English border.
878	Death of Rhodri Fawr, first Welsh ruler to unite most of Wales.
927	Weakened by Viking attacks, Welsh kings forced to pay homage to English.
1039	Gruffudd ap Llywelyn becomes king of whole of Wales.
1063	Harold of England invades Wales. Llywelyn killed by his own men.
1066	Norman invasion of England, pushing on into Wales.
1200	Llywelyn I leads national uprising.
1267	Llywelyn II secures Treaty of Montgomery with England, recognising Welsh independence.
1282	England's Edward I brutally invades and conquers Wales, declaring it an English principality. Llywelyn II killed.
1301	Edward invests his son as Prince of Wales.
1349	Black Death kills up to 40% of Welsh population.
1400	Owain Glyndŵr leads national uprising against England.
1410	Glyndŵr defeated and subsequently disappeared.. Humiliating anti-Welsh laws imposed.
1455	War of the Roses. Welsh support Henry Tudor.
1485	Succession of Welshman Henry Tudor to the throne of England after victory at the Battle of Bosworth.
1536	Henry VIII enforces Act of Union, ensuring complete political and legal annexation to England.
1588	Bible published in Welsh.
1642	English Civil War. On gaining power, Cromwell imposes his rule over the Welsh.

1660	Restoration of monarchy and end of Cromwellian protectorate welcomed by Welsh.
1718	Introduction of printing press in Wales, publishing increasing number of books in Welsh language.
1735	Beginning of Methodist revival.
1782	David Williams publishes revolutionary treatise 'Letters on Political Liberty'.
1787	Attempted invasion by French.
1794	Morgan John Rhys leads group of emigrants to America in attempt to establish Welsh-speaking community.
1795	South Wales iron industry expands.
1820s-1830s	'Scotch Cattle' activities by miners against unpopular managers and blacklegs.
1831	Merthyr Rising, suppressed by troops and ending with the execution of Dic Penderyn.
1839	Rebecca Riots begin. Toll gates destroyed.
1839	Chartist disturbances, culminating in 'Battle of Newport' and the transportation of leading activists.
1847	'Blue Books' educational report condemns Welsh language.
1850s	South Wales coal industry rapidly expands.
1856	'Mae Hen Wlad fy Nhadau' (Land of my Fathers), Wales' national anthem, composed.
1865	Michael D. Jones leads emigrant party to Argentina, where their Welsh-speaking descendants still live.
1868	Liberal Party becomes dominant in Wales.
1887-1891	'Tithe War' protest against payment of tithes to Anglican Church.
1898	South Wales Miners Federation formed.
1900	Wales' (and Britain's) first Labour MP, James Keir Hardie, becomes MP for Merthyr.
1908	David Lloyd George becomes Chancellor of the Exchequer, introducing old age pensions.
1900-1903	Bethesda slate quarry strike.
1910	Tonypandy riots. Troops brought in to quell miners.
1914	Anglican Church disestablished in Wales.

1914-1918	World War I.
1922	Lloyd George, Prime Minister since 1916, steps down. Liberal Party declines, the Labour Party to become the new dominant party of Wales.
1925	Plaid Cymru formed.
1926	General Strike.
1930s	Depression hits South Wales coalfield. In some places, unemployment exceeds 30%.
1936	Plaid Cymru set fire to R.A.F. bombing station near Cricieth, Llŷn.
1937	South Wales Regional Council of Labour formed, later to become Wales Labour Party.
1939-1945	World War II.
1955	Cardiff officially declared capital.
1960s	Bombing and sabotage on dams by rural extremists.
1962	Cymdeithas yr laith Gymraeg (Welsh Language Society) founded.
1964	Appointment of Secretary of State for Wales.
1966	Gwynfor Evans elected First Plaid Cymru MP.
1979	Welsh reject devolution in referendum.
1982	Welsh TV channel, S4C, begins broadcasting.
1984-1985	National Miners' Strike against pit closures.
1997	Referendum on Welsh Assembly. Narrow majority in favour.
1999	Opening of Welsh Assembly, Cardiff.

famous welsh people

cinema

Richard Burton
Sir Anthony Hopkins
Glynis John
Hywel Bennet
Hugh Griffith
Alex Jenkins
Desmond Llewelyn
Catherine Zeta-Jones

exploration

Edgar Evans (Antarctica)
Thomas Jones (The Arctic)
Sir Henry Morgan (buccaneer)
John Evans (The Missouri)
John Lloyd (America)
Henry Morton Stanley (Africa)

literature

Daffyd ap Gwilym
W.H. Davies
George Herbert
Saunders Lewis
R. Williams Parry
Kate Roberts
R.S. Thomas
Roald Dahl
Caradoc Evans (David Evans)
T. Gwyn Jones
Richard Llewellyn
Sir Thomas Parry
Dylan Thomas
Sir Thomas Parry Williams

military

T.E. Lawrence ('Lawrence of Arabia')

music/opera/theatre

Ivor Emmanuel
Alun Hoddinott
Dame Gwyneth Jones
Margaret Price
Sir Geraint Evans
Aled Jones
Joseph Parry
Emlyn Williams

popular music

The Alarm
Catatonia
Manic Street Preachers
Steve Strange
Shirley Bassey
Mary Hopkin
Stereophonics
Super Furry Animals

politics

Aneurin Bevan
Gwynfor Evans
Cledwyn Hughes
Sir John Harvey Jones
Rhodri Morgan
Clement Davies
David Lloyd George
Roy Jenkins
Neil Kinnock
Viscount Tonypandy

social philosophy

Robert Owen
Bertrand Russell

sport

David Broome (show jumping)
Gareth Edwards (rugby union)
Ryan Giggs (football)
Terry Griffiths (snooker)
Debbie Johnsey (show jumping)
Ray Reardon (snooker)
J.P.R. Williams (rugby union)
Lyn Davies (athletics)
Alan Evans (darts)
Sandra Greatbach (darts)
Colin Jackson (athletics)
Doug Mountjoy (snooker)
Jim Sullivan (rugby league)
Ian Woosnam (golf)

television

Max Boyce
Kenneth Griffith
Sian Lloyd
Sir Harry Secombe
Windsor Davies
Griff Rhys Jones
Ruth Madoc

visual arts

Augustus John
Ceri Richards
Gwen John
Kiffin Williams

bibliography

history

John Davies — **A History of Wales**
Penguin, 1994

Peter Berresford Ellis — **Wales: a Nation Again!**
Tandem, n.d.

D. Gareth Evans — **A History of Wales 1815-1906**
University of Wales Press, 1993

Gwynfor Evans — **Land of My Fathers**
Y Lolfa, 1992

Trevor Fishlock — **Talking of Wales**
Cassell, n.d.

Trevor Fishlock — **Wales and the Welsh**
Cassell, n.d.

Gerald of Wales, Lewis Thorpe (tr) — **The Journey Through Wales/The Description of Wales**
Penguin, 1978

Philip Jenkins — **A History of Modern Wales 1536-1990**
Longman, 1990

Gareth Elwyn Jones — **Modern Wales: a concise history**
Cambridge University Press, 1994

Kenneth O. Morgan — **Rebirth of a Nation: a history of modern Wales**
Oxford University Press, 1989

Jan Morris — **The Matter of Wales**
Oxford University Press, 1986

Ned Thomas — **The Welsh Extremist**
Y Lolfa, 1991

Wynford Vaughan Thomas — **Wales: a History**
Michael Joseph, 1985

David Walker — **Mediaeval Wales**
Cambridge University Press, 1990

Gwyn A. Williams — **When was Wales?**
Penguin, 1985

Hugh Williams (tr) — **Two Lives of Gildas**
Llanerch, 1990

language

Janet Davies — **The Welsh Language**
University of Wales Press, 1993

literature & arts

Joseph Clancy (tr) — **Twentieth Century Welsh Poems**
Dufour Editions, 1982

Patrick K. Ford (ed) — **Ystoria Taliesin: The Story of Taliesin**
University of Wales Press, 1992

R. Geraint Gruffydd (ed) — **Cerddi Saunders Lewis**
University of Wales Press, 1986

Thomas Parry — **A History of Welsh Literature**
Oxford University Press, 1955

Thomas Parry — **Hanes Llenyddiaeth Gymraeg hyg 1900**
University of Wales Press, 1993

Meirion Pennar (tr) — **Taliesin Poems**
Llanerch, 1988

Meirion Pennar (tr) — **The Black Book of Carmarthen**
Llanerch, 1989

Steve Short (tr) — **Aneirin: The Gododdin**
Llanerch, 1994

Meic Stephens (ed) — **Cydymaith i Lenyddiaeth Cymru**
University of Wales Press, 1993

religion

J.W. James (ed) — **Rhigyfarch's Life of St David**
University of Wales Press, 1985

Stuart Piggott — **The Druids**
Thames & Hudson, 1985

Glanmor Williams — **The Welsh and their Religion: Historical Essays**
University of Wales Press, 1991

modern wales

Kenneth O. Morgan — **Modern Wales: Politics, Places and People**
University of Wales Press, 1995

index

JEFF FALLOW is a freelance illustrator and graphic designer living in Fife. He illustrated **Stanislavski for Beginners™**, and **London For Beginners ™**. He is the author and illustrator of **Scotland for Beginners ™**. He is also a political cartoonist, with work published in *CND Today* and *Scots Independent*.